How to access your on-line resources

Kaplan Financial students will have a MyKaplan account and these extra resources will be available to you online. You do not need to register again, as this process was completed when you enrolled. If you are having problems accessing online materials, please ask your course administrator.

If you are not studying with Kaplan and did not purchase your book via a Kaplan website, to unlock your extra online resources please go to www.en-gage.co.uk (even if you have set up an account and registered books previously). You will then need to enter the ISBN number (on the title page and back cover) and the unique pass key number contained in the scratch panel below to gain access.

You will also be required to enter additional information during this process to set up or confirm your account details.

If you purchased through the Kaplan Publishing website you will automatically receive an e-mail invitation to register your details and gain access to your content. If you do not receive the e-mail or book content, please contact Kaplan Publishing.

Your code and information

This code can only be used once for the registration of one book online. This registration and your online content will expire when the final sittings for the examinations covered by this book have taken place. Please allow one hour from the time you submit your book details for us to process your request.

Please scratch the film to access your unique code.

Please be aware that this code is case-sensitive and you will need to include the dashes within the passcode, but not when entering the ISBN.

CIMA

Case Study

Management Level

Study Text

Published by: Kaplan Publishing UK

Unit 2 The Business Centre, Molly Millars Lane, Wokingham, Berkshire RG41 2QZ

Acknowledgements

"We are grateful to the CIMA for permission to reproduce past examination questions and the official CIMA answers

Notice

The text in this material and any others made available by any Kaplan Group company does not amount to advice on a particular matter and should not be taken as such. No reliance should be placed on the content as the basis for any investment or other decision or in connection with any advice given to third parties. Please consult your appropriate professional adviser as necessary.

Kaplan Publishing Limited and all other Kaplan group companies expressly disclaim all liability to any person in respect of any losses or other claims, whether direct, indirect, incidental, consequential or otherwise arising in relation to the use of such materials.

Kaplan is not responsible for the content of external websites. The inclusion of a link to a third party website in this text should not be taken as an endorsement.

Kaplan Publishing's learning materials are designed to help students succeed in their examinations. In certain circumstances, CIMA can make post-exam adjustment to a student's mark or grade to reflect adverse circumstances which may have disadvantaged a student's ability to take an exam or demonstrate their normal level of attainment (see CIMA's Special Consideration policy). However, it should be noted that students will not be eligible for special consideration by CIMA if preparation for or performance in a CIMA exam is affected by any failure by their tuition provider to prepare them properly for the exam for any reason including, but not limited to, staff shortages, building work or a lack of facilities etc.

Similarly, CIMA will not accept applications for special consideration on any of the following grounds:

- failure by a tuition provider to cover the whole syllabus
- failure by the student to cover the whole syllabus, for instance as a result of joining a course part way through
- failure by the student to prepare adequately for the exam, or to use the correct pre-seen material
- errors in the Kaplan Official Study Text, including sample (practice) questions or any other Kaplan content or
- errors in any other study materials (from any other tuition provider or publisher).

British Library Cataloguing in Publication Data

A catalogue record for this book is available from the British Library.

ISBN: 978-1-78740-986-6

Printed and bound in Great Britain

Contents

Introduction

Acknowledgements

Every effort has been made to contact the holders of copyright material, but if any here have been inadvertently overlooked the publishers will be pleased to make the necessary arrangements at the first opportunity.

How to use the Materials

Test your understanding – Following key points and definitions are exercises which give the opportunity to assess the understanding of these core areas. Within the work book the answers to these sections are left blank, explanations to the questions can be found within the online version which can be hidden or shown on screen to enable repetition of activities.

Illustration – to help develop an understanding of topics and the test your understanding exercises the illustrative examples can be used.

Quality and accuracy are of the utmost importance to us so if you spot an error in any of our products, please send an email to mykaplanreporting@kaplan.com with full details.

Our Quality Coordinator will work with our technical team to verify the error and take action to ensure it is corrected in future editions.

Exam Introduction

To complete the CIMA qualification and be able to use the designatory letters of ACMA and CGMA, candidates for this prestigious award need to achieve three things:

- attain the entry requirements for the professional level qualification
- study for and complete the relevant professional level assessments and examinations
- complete three years of relevant practical experience

This text concentrates on the second of these requirements, and in particular to study for and complete the Management level case study exam.

Overview of exam

The case study exam will be available four times a year. The purpose of this exam is to consolidate learning at each level by reflecting real life work situations. The exam is human marked.

This approach allows a wide range of knowledge and skills to be tested including research and analysis, presentation of information and communication skills whilst still ensuring competence in key skills.

CIMA believe that this format will provide the commitment to delivering the competencies which employers' desire thereby improving 'employability'.

For example, the Management level case study exam will be set within a simulated business context, placing the candidate in the job role matched to the competency level. In the case of the Management level, the job role is that of a Financial Manager (usually a management accountant) with responsibility for monitoring and implementing strategy. The focus will be on the need to translate long-term decisions into medium-term plans.

Typical aspects of such a role could include the following:

- Responsibility for monitoring and implementing strategy, focussing on the medium term. Translating the long-term strategy that has been decided at the senior management/board level into medium-term, tactical goals.
- Making full use of technologies to derive information that can be of value in evaluating business opportunities, including the implementation of cyber technologies in order to evaluate business processes and to create and enhance value for the company
- Collaboration with colleagues from finance and other disciplines to make decisions concerning investment projects, product development and product pricing.
- A sound understanding of the business environment, including the opportunities arising in the digital ecosystem, and a requirement to measure and report on the performance of individuals and divisions and an expectation to evaluate business risks
- Involvement in the accounting decisions that affect the preparation and content of the consolidated financial statements prepared by the company, requiring the exercise of professional judgement taking into account the effect that recommendations and decisions can have on the actions of internal and external decision-makers.
- Strong communication skills. The need to inform key decisions may raise significant ethical dilemmas that must be resolved in a justifiable and professional manner.

The exam is intended to replicate "a day in the life" of a finance professional operating at the Management level and provide a simulated environment for candidates to demonstrate the required level of proficiency in each of the competency areas. Consequently, the exam will be set and marked according to the weightings for each core activity.

The case study exam is 3 hours in duration and is made up of a series of timed tests or tasks. This makes the case study exam different from most exams you will have sat to date – once you have submitted a particular task (or the time limit is reached, whichever is sooner) you will be moved on and will not be able to return to that task. This should reduce the problem of not completing the paper but does mean you will need to be very disciplined when attempting each task.

Candidates will be provided with access to pre-seen information approximately seven weeks before the real exam.

Assessment aims and strategy

The Case Study Examination tests the knowledge, skills and techniques from the three pillars within one simulated scenario and is taken at the end of each level of the CIMA Professional Qualification. Candidates are given a fictional Case Study before the examination and are expected to give solutions to the situations and challenges presented within the examination – based on the knowledge and skills acquired from the three pillars. The Case Study mimics their role in a real-work scenario, at each level of the qualification.

The case study exam is three hours long. The case study will include both pre-seen and unseen material, the latter being made available during the examination. The unseen materials will provide additional information, possibly in the form of emails, news reports and other formats. They will also include the tasks (or requirements).

They will incorporate short written answers, emails, letters and any form of appropriate communication required within the tasks set.

The focus is on application, analysis and evaluation which are levels 3, 4 and 5 of the CIMA hierarchy of verbs (see below).

Simulated business issues in the case studies provide candidates with the opportunity to demonstrate their familiarity with the context and interrelationships of the level's technical content. This reflects the cross functional abilities required in the workplace. Skills will include research, analysis, and the presentation of both financial and nonfinancial information and communication skills.

Feedback will be provided to candidates with their results.

Exam sittings for the case studies will occur every three months.

Candidates must have completed or be exempt from the three objective tests at a particular level before attempting the case study at that level.

Core activities and assessment outcomes

Within each Management Case Study Examination, five "core activities" will be assessed. These core activities represent the tasks that are most frequent, critical and important to the entry level finance professional role.

The five core activities are:

A Evaluate opportunities to add value.

B Implement senior management decisions.

C Manage performance and costs to aid value creation.

D Measure performance.

E Manage internal and external stakeholders.

The core activities are linked to associated assessment outcomes expressed in terms of 'I Can' statements that speak directly to the skills and competencies that drive the employability of successful learners.

The core activities require and draw together the knowledge, skills and techniques acquired while studying for Objective Tests and combining them with the mind-set of a CIMA finance professional.

Each core activity is translated into a number of "assessment outcomes". These are a clear assertion of what a CIMA qualified finance professional should be able to do when the Examination has been completed and what the assessment will be designed to measure. Case Study assessment outcomes will be synoptic.

The synoptic case study style exam will assess the candidate's ability to analyse and respond to a typical set of business-related tasks through a simulation that reflects activities undertaken in a typical role at this level of competence.

At the Management level, the role simulated is that of a financial manager. The Case Study Examination provides a simulated context allowing candidates to demonstrate that they have acquired the required knowledge, skills, techniques and the mind-set required for that role.

These are discussed in more detail in chapters 1 and 2

Assessing skills – the CIMA verb hierarchy

CIMA has adopted a skill framework for the assessments based on the revised Bloom's Taxonomy of Education Objectives. Bloom's Taxonomy classifies a continuum of skills that learners are expected to know and demonstrate.

The case study exam will focus on Levels 3, 4 and 5.

Skill level	Verbs used	Definition
Level 5 Evaluation How you are expected to use your learning to evaluate, make decisions or recommendations	Advise	Counsel, inform or notify
	Assess	Evaluate or estimate the nature, ability or quality of
	Evaluate	Appraise or assess the value of
	Recommend	Propose a course of action
	Review	Assess and evaluate in order, to change if necessary
Level 4 Analysis How you are expected to analyse the detail of what you have learned	Align	Arrange in an orderly way
	Analyse	Examine in detail the structure of
	Communicate	Share or exchange information
	Compare and contrast	Show the similarities and/or differences between
	Develop	Grow and expand a concept
	Discuss	Examine in detail by argument
	Examine	Inspect thoroughly
	Interpret	Translate into intelligible or familiar terms
	Monitor	Observe and check the progress of
	Prioritise	Place in order of priority or sequence for action
	Produce	Create or bring into existence
Level 3 Application How you are expected to apply your knowledge	Apply	Put to practical use
	Calculate	Ascertain or reckon mathematically
	Conduct	Organise and carry out
	Demonstrate	Prove with certainty or exhibit by practical means
	Prepare	Make or get ready for use
	Reconcile	Make or prove consistent/compatible
Level 2 Comprehension What you are expected to understand	Describe	Communicate the key features of
	Distinguish	Highlight the differences between
	Explain	Make clear or intelligible/state the meaning or purpose of
	Identify	Recognise, establish or select after consideration
	Illustrate	Use an example to describe or explain something
Level 1 Knowledge What you are expected to know	List	Make a list of
	State	Express, fully or clearly, the details/facts of
	Define	Give the exact meaning of
	Outline	Give a summary of

How to use the material

These Official CIMA learning materials brought to you by CIMA and Kaplan Publishing have been carefully designed to make your learning experience as easy as possible and give you the best chances of success in your Case Study Examinations.

This Study Text has been designed with the needs of home study and distance learning candidates in mind. However, the Study Text is also ideal for fully taught courses.

The aim of this textbook is to walk you through the stages to prepare for, and to answer, the requirements of the Case Study Examination.

Practical hints and realistic tips are given throughout the book making it easy for you to apply what you've learned in this text to your actual Case Study Exam.

Where sample solutions are provided, they must be viewed as just one interpretation of the case. One key aspect, which you must appreciate early in your studies, is that there is no single 'correct' solution.

Your own answer might reach different conclusions, and give greater emphasis to some issues and less emphasis to others, but score equally as well if it demonstrates the required skills.

If you work conscientiously through the official CIMA Study Text according to the guidelines above, as well as analysing the pre-seen information in full, you will be giving yourself an excellent chance of success in your examination.

In addition, it is important to remind candidates to work through the technical material, of the three pillars underpinning the case study examination where particular weaknesses in understanding have been identified.

This is especially relevant if candidates passed a particular OTQ in the distant past or they were exempt it from previous study.

Good luck with your studies!

Planning

To begin with, formal planning is essential to get the best return from the time you spend studying. Estimate how much time in total you are going to need for each subject you are studying for the Case Study Examination.

This book will provide you with proven study techniques. Chapter by chapter it covers the building blocks of successful learning and examination techniques and shows you how to earn all the marks you deserve, and explains how to avoid the most common pitfalls.

With your study material before you, decide which chapters you are going to study in each week, which weeks you will devote to practising past exams, and which weeks you will spend becoming familiar with your case study pre-seen material.

Prepare a written schedule summarising the above and stick to it! Students are advised to refer to articles published regularly in CIMA's magazine (Financial Management), the student e-newsletter (Velocity) and on the CIMA website, to ensure they are up to date with relevant issues and topics.

Tips for effective studying

1. Aim to find a quiet and undisturbed location for your study, and plan as far as possible to use the same period of time each day. Getting into a routine helps to avoid wasting time. Make sure that you have all the materials you need before you begin so as to minimise interruptions.
2. Store all your materials in one place, so that you do not waste time searching for items every time you want to begin studying. If you have to pack everything away after each study period, keep your study materials in a box, or even a suitcase, which will not be disturbed until the next time.
3. Limit distractions. To make the most effective use of your study periods you should be able to apply total concentration, so turn off all entertainment equipment, set your phones to message mode, and put up your 'do not disturb' sign.
4. Your timetable will tell you which topic to study. However, before diving in and becoming engrossed in the finer points, make sure you have an overall picture of all the areas that need to be covered by the end of that session. After an hour, allow yourself a short break and move away from your Study Text. With experience, you will learn to assess the pace you need to work at. Each study session should focus on component learning outcomes – the basis for all questions.
5. Work carefully through a chapter, making notes as you go. When you have covered a suitable amount of material, vary the pattern by attempting a practice question. When you have finished your attempt, make notes of any mistakes you made, or any areas that you failed to cover or covered more briefly. Be aware that all component learning outcomes will be tested in each examination.
6. Make notes as you study, and discover the techniques that work best for you. Your notes may be in the form of lists, bullet points, diagrams, summaries, 'mind maps', or the written word, but remember that you will need to refer back to them at a later date, so they must be intelligible. If you are on a taught course, make sure you highlight any issues you would like to follow up with your lecturer.
7. Organise your notes. Make sure that all your notes, calculations etc. can be effectively filed and easily retrieved later.

Relevant practical experience

In order to become a Chartered Global Management Accountant (ACMA, CGMA), you need a minimum of three years' verified relevant work-based practical experience.

Read the 'Applying for Membership' brochure for full details of the practical experience requirements (PER).

Information concerning formulae and tables will be provided via the CIMA website, www.cimaglobal.com.

Chapter

1

Introduction to case study exams

Chapter learning objectives

- To gain an overview of the case study exam, its purpose, structure and the process involved.

1 The structure of the CIMA Management Level

Each level of CIMA's professional qualification consists of three objective test 'pillar' exams, followed by the Case Study Examination.

You can only attempt the Case Study Examination after all objective tests for the level have been completed or if exemptions have been given.

For the 2019 syllabus the three Management level pillar exams are as follows:

- E2 – Managing Performance
- P2 – Advanced Management Accounting
- F2 – Advanced Financial Reporting

The objective tests for each of these individual subjects ensure the acquisition of the breadth of knowledge, skills and techniques that provide the foundation for approaching the Case Study Examination.

2 Why a Case Study Examination?

The CIMA Case Study Examinations are 'capstone' examinations designed to demonstrate mastery of previously acquired knowledge, skills and techniques and the drawing together of these to provide solutions to unstructured, synoptic problems.

Each synoptic assessment combines the content covered in all three pillar subjects at the level into a single assessment. Its aim is the "undoing" of the pillar and subject divisions of the syllabus and the application of knowledge, skills and techniques to the type of problems that you might encounter in the workplace in a role matched to the appropriate level of the qualification.

The examination uses a simulated Case Study to provide a rich, immersive scenario to prepare and to provide a context for the tasks in the examination. The case study scenarios are developed around today's modern business environment and the challenges that you will face – allowing you to demonstrate the 'core activities' that have been identified by employers as critical.

The tasks within the unseen examination will be practical and applied, not theoretical or academic. To be successful, you will have to perform these core activities in the same way and to the same standards that would be valid and valued in the workplace.

The Case Study Examination is thus an attempt to simulate workplace problem solving, and allows examiners to move one step closer to the assessment of competence than is possible with objective test questions. It is a test of both professional competence and, by implication, employability.

In addition, the purpose of the Case Study Examination is to assess your proficiency in those specific skills that are less likely to be automated.

The purpose of this text is to suggest how you might prepare for the examination by developing and practising your skills. Since the examination tests a range of different skills, preparing for this examination needs to be different from studying for a 'traditional' examination.

3 Your role

Each case study examination will be set within a simulated business context, placing the candidate in the job role matched to the competency level.

In the case of the Management level the role simulated is that of a Financial Manager, reporting to the Financial Controller, Finance Director, Board Members and/or peers within the organisation

This role can be broken down as follows:

- As a manager with responsibility for monitoring and implementing strategy the job focus is on the medium term. This involves translating the long-term strategy that has been decided at the senior management/board level into medium-term, tactical goals, making full use of technologies to derive information that can be of value in evaluating business opportunities, including the implementation of cyber technologies in order to evaluate business processes and to create and enhance value for the company
- The manager has to collaborate with colleagues from finance and other disciplines to make decisions concerning investment projects, product development and product pricing and relies on the output of junior colleagues on matters such as cost drivers to formulate optimal recommendations. The responsibilities require a sound understanding of the business environment, including the opportunities arising in the digital ecosystem, and the manager is required to measure and report on the performance of individuals and divisions. There is also an expectation to evaluate business risks
- Being involved in the accounting decisions that affect the preparation and content of the consolidated financial statements prepared by the company, the manager's duties require the exercise of professional judgement, as recommendations and decisions can have a significant impact on the actions of both internal and external decision-makers. The manager's successful performance requires strong communication skills. The need to inform key decisions may raise significant ethical dilemmas that must be resolved in a justifiable and professional manner.

In summary, the Management level focuses on the skills the Finance Manager will need to translate long-term decisions into medium-term plans. In the same way as a finance professional working at this level, candidates will be able to use data and relevant technology to manage organisational and individual performance, allocate resources to implement decisions; monitor and report implementation of decisions; as well as prepare and interpret financial statements to show performance, among other responsibilities.

The competency level assesses you on five core activities that are the most frequent, important and critical to the work of the finance manager. These include evaluating opportunities to add value, implementing senior management decisions, managing performance and costs to aid value creation, measuring performance and managing internal and external stakeholders.

4 The exam 'blueprints'

For the first time, CIMA has released blueprints for its Professional Qualification Examination. The intent is that blueprints will demystify the examination – giving greater clarity on examinable topics; assessment approach, design and weightings; and learner expectations.

The Case Study Examination blueprint contains the following:

- **Core activities** – Business-related tasks that are common to the role being simulated and valued by employers which, if performed satisfactorily, enables the demonstration of the assessment outcomes.
- **Assessment outcomes** – A clear assertion of what a CIMA qualified finance professional can do when the examination has been completed and what the assessment will be designed to measure. Case Study assessment outcomes will be synoptic.

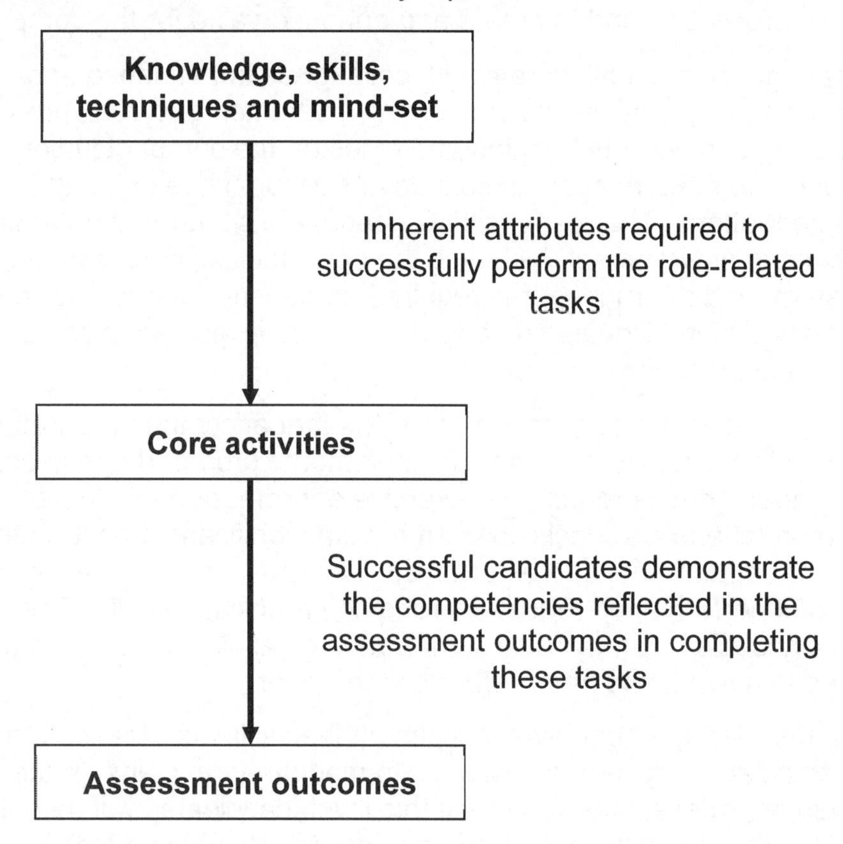

All core activities will be assessed in each form of the examination in line with the weightings. A sample of related assessment outcomes will be tested.

Blueprints are discussed in more detail in chapter 2.

5 The exam process

5.1 Overview

The examination is three hours long. A 15-minute tutorial is available before the start of the examination to allow candidates to familiarise themselves with the test driver.

The examination has four sections (tasks), which are each 45 minutes long. All sections are equally weighted. Candidates may finish a section early and move on to the next but cannot return to previous sections in the time remaining.

There may be more than one sub-task within each section and an indication of how long to spend on each sub-task will be given to allow candidates to manage their time.

For example, the first exam variant of the sample prototype paper shows the following instructions:

Section (task)	Time for section (minutes)	Number of answer screens	Number of sub-tasks	% time to spend on each sub-task
1	45	1	2	(a) 50% (b) 50%
2	45	1	2	(a) 60% (b) 40%
3	45	1	2	(a) 40% (b) 60%
4	45	1	2	(a) 50% (b) 50%

More than one core activity will normally (but not always) be assessed in each section/task and the order of core activities and assessment outcomes in the blueprint does not reflect how these might be structured in the examination.

For each sitting there are a number of variants, so different students will not necessarily face the same exam tasks. You are not permitted to discuss any aspects of the variant you sat until after the exam window has finished. The marking and moderation processes ensure that no advantage is gained from sitting one particular variant rather than another.

5.2 The pre-seen

The exam is based on:

- pre-seen material issued in advance of the exam day, supplemented by
- additional, previously unseen material given to you in the exam room.

From the May 2020 sitting onwards, one pre-seen will be used over two exam windows, giving candidates the opportunity to resit using the same pre-seen. The pre-seen will be shared as follows:

- May / August
- November / February

CIMA releases the pre-seen material approximately seven weeks before the first examination. This is posted on the student area of the CIMA website (www.cimaglobal.com) and it is your responsibility to download it and to print off a copy.

The pre-seen material is an introductory scenario to set the scene for the case study, together with accounting and financial information. The pre-seen material is an extended scenario, which contains a range of background sections and a maximum of 4 or 5 exhibits, with additional information which may or not be specific to the organisation itself.

You will be taking on the role of a Finance Manager who works for the organisation, and your responses to the tasks will usually be addressed to your superior.

5.3 The unseen

In the examination you will be provided with the following.

- An on-screen version of the pre-seen material
- Additional new unseen material, which contains both triggers (new information) and tasks (what you need to do)
- Space to complete your answers
- An on-screen calculator (although candidates are permitted to take their own calculators as long as it's a CIMA approved model.)
- Reference materials (Present value tables, Cumulative present value tables and Normal distribution tables)
- A notepad and pen for planning and workings along with an on-screen scratch pad.

The unseen material will be a continuation of the pre-seen and will usually bring the scenario up to date. In some cases there is a 'twist' in the unseen i.e. a development that students might not have anticipated from the pre-seen. The unseen may focus on a number of issues that appeared in the pre-seen or it may just focus on one or two; either way it will provide the basis for the content of your answers.

A common mistake made by weaker students is that they place too much emphasis on their analysis of the pre-seen material and do not develop the information in the unseen material adequately. The key points to be referred to in your answer should be driven by the new information in the unseen material.

5.4 Triggers and tasks

Each section in the unseen material will begin with a **trigger.**

This will be information provided as an introduction to the work that you are required to complete.

The information may be in the form of a briefing by your superior, a newspaper article, some financial information or extracts from internal reports. You will be expected to integrate this new information with the analysis you have performed on the pre-seen material to produce a coherent and well informed response.

Within each section of the examination, there will then be a **task** or tasks that you will be asked to perform, usually by your superior. These tasks will require different types of response, although usually reports, briefing notes and emails.

Word processing capabilities will be provided within the test driver to allow the formatting and presentation of responses in a professional manner. From 2019, this includes the ability to use tables to put together a response. For full details of the word processing functionality and to try this in advance of the examination, a tutorial is available on cimaglobal.com.

There is a time limit attached to each task and you will have a clock showing the time remaining in the corner of your screen. Once you have submitted a task (or the time limit is reached, whichever is sooner) you will not be able to return to that task. This should reduce the problem of not completing the paper but does mean you will need to be disciplined when attempting each task.

If you feel that you do not need all of the time on an earlier task, then moving forwards prematurely will not allow you extra time on later tasks – the extra time will be lost. Given this, it is always advisable to use the full time allocated to each task to recheck that you have answered the question requirement in full and that you have related your response to the specific context of the case.

A walkthrough of the prototype sample exam will be carried out in chapters 3 to 5.

5.5 Calculations

Examination tasks will not be set that require specific calculations.

However, candidates should, wherever possible, show how they have used and interpreted data from the pre-seen and the new information presented during the examination and/or undertook analysis or calculations to support their responses.

6 Marking

6.1 'Three level' marking

The Case Study Examinations are human marked using a holistic 'three level' approach for each task, enabling markers to give credit for all relevant points, even if not mentioned in the indicative answer.

For example, in the February 2020 exam, Task 1(a) of Variant 1, worth 13 marks, asked candidates to do the following:

"How would the release of a significant proportion of our back catalogue on vinyl affect Trevel's value chain?"

The published indicative answer was accompanied by the following marking grid

Trait			
Defining changes	**Level**	**Descriptor**	**Marks**
		No rewardable material	0
	Level 1	Offers a brief overview of changes to the value chain	1
	Level 2	Offers a clear overview of changes to the value chain	2-3
	Level 3	Offers a clear and full overview of changes to the value chain	4
Trait			
Impacts on the value chain	**Level**	**Descriptor**	**Marks**
		No rewardable material	0
	Level 1	Offers a limited discussion of the impacts on the value chain 1–3	1–3
	Level 2	Offers a clear discussion of the impacts on the value chain.	4–6
	Level 3	Offers a clear and comprehensive discussion of the impacts on the value chain	7–9

The lessons to be learned

The key differences between the levels are

- Number of points made.
- Degree of application to the context of the pre-seen and/or scenario.
- The extent to which you answered the question set – in this case "how would the release of a significant proportion of our back catalogue **on vinyl affect Trevel's value chain".**

Make sure your answers address these issues.

NB:

It is important to reiterate that candidates must **read the questions carefully** and answer them as fully and directly as possible in the time available.

Similarly, candidates are reminded that they must **answer the question as set**.

In this context, candidates can be reassured that markers are under very specific instructions to accept **any relevant and correct points** made in the script.

6.2 The 'marginally competent' candidate

CIMA have disclosed further information on how the pass mark is set and the importance of identifying the 'marginally competent' student.

The process

A detailed process was revealed that involves the following:

(1) A panel of experts debates the tasks within a variant to decide what should be expected from a student deemed competent for this task. This debate does not focus on a perfect answer but, instead, asks what would be expected of a CIMA student (or member) in practice – what is the minimum expected if we were considering employing them, for example.

(2) A sample of student scripts is then discussed and the scripts ranked. This is repeated and refined until the "marginally competent student" is identified. This student deserves to pass (but only just!) as they would be employable and have the skills expected of a CIMA student or member in the real world.

(3) The marks earned by this script are then used to set the pass mark and standardise the overall marking system. This ensures that students are not disadvantaged if they sit a "harder" variant.

The lessons to be learned

When answering a task in the exam, you could imagine that this was part of a job interview and ask yourself what would be required to get the job.

Your employer would be less impressed by you showing off knowledge but much more impressed that you can answer a question asked, apply your comments to the company's specific circumstances and make practical, relevant suggestions. Make sure your answers do this!

Demonstrating soft skills

In an article written for CIMA's website, the examiners made the following comments on the need for candidates to demonstrate so-called 'soft skills':

In a role simulation exam, it is critical that the candidate inhabits the role and the scenario in order to perform as well as possible. Applying technical knowledge and skills gained to the scenario together with the professional or "soft" skills that are critical for success in the workplace will enable candidates to demonstrate that they have achieved the core activities set out in the blueprint and can apply these in the context of the business, providing the best responses to the tasks.

These professional or soft skills are useful in any professional setting and include skills such as:

- *Communication*
- *Awareness of the digital ecosystem*
- *Professional scepticism*
- *Provide leadership*
- *Professional judgement*
- *Ethics and professionalism*
- *Business awareness.*

These skills are not tested directly (and marks are not specifically allocated to them), but they should be drawn upon when developing an answer plan. Applying these skills will support you in responding to a task and aid you in producing an answer that is relevant, provides the best solution for the simulated organisation and the issues it is facing and, consequently, achieves the highest marks available (that is, meeting the level 3 descriptors in the marking guides).

Questions need not necessarily – and likely will not – refer to a specific mind-set skill in order to make it relevant. For example, a question might summarise a subordinate's explanation for a disappointing performance. A good candidate might apply professional scepticism in evaluating the validity of the explanation. If the question asks for a recommended response then the candidate might consider the leadership issues associated with alternatives. In some circumstances a reprimand might be in order and in others it might be preferable to offer support and encouragement.

Mind-set and soft skills can be developed through practice. Reflecting on personal experiences at work, reading the business news and even attempting past case study exams are all ways to develop an understanding of what might work in any given set of circumstances.

6.3 A scaled score

Incorporating the 'marginally competent' student exercise and to ensure equity between exam variants, your mark will be adjusted to give a 'scaled score' out of 150 with 80 and above being a pass.

6.4 Feedback and 'grade descriptors'

Feedback on performance against each core activity will be provided so that learners know their areas of weakness for further study. (Note: there is no requirement to obtain a pass or meet a minimum threshold for each core activity – it is the overall mark that matters.)

In addition to the wording of core activities and assessment objectives, CIMA has published 'grade descriptors' to give you more insight into the skills required to pass. It is these that are used to feedback performance to students.

For example, the grade descriptors for core activity A are as follows

Core activity	**Assessment outcome**	*If you met the exam level passing standard for each of the core activities, you can generally be described using some or all of the following characteristics:*
A. Evaluate opportuniti es to add value	1. I can select appropriate capital investment appraisal techniques and apply them in order to support capital investment decisions, including product/ service development, digital transformation projects and acquisitions. 2. I can identify and use relevant digital data sources to assist in capital investment decisions. 3. I can explain which pricing strategies are appropriate. 4. I can select and implement suitable business models that will create value for stakeholders, including business models in the context of digital ecosystems. 5. I can analyse the impact of disruptive and digital operating business models in the context of digital ecosystems. 6. I can explain the relevance of weighted average cost of capital.	• Demonstrates technical understanding of the models and techniques that are used to add value. • Communicates business recommendations and their justification clearly. • Applies professional judgement in offering advice and recommendations to senior management. • Demonstrates understanding of the business model and its environment, including digital ecosystems and disruptive businesses, and can support senior management in decision making. • Applies professional scepticism to the evaluation of opportunities and the evaluation of proposals. • Demonstrates business awareness in selecting and applying techniques and models with a view to adding value.

Note that the verbs used in the third column (grade descriptors) are different from those in the second (assessment outcomes). This is designed to show how the 'softer skills' enable and support the achievements of the assessment outcomes and core activities within the simulation. It's intended to draw out the importance of these skills to support producing the best, most applied and plausible answers within the simulation.

The two columns are complementary and should be read in conjunction.

If in the exam, you score enough marks for the tasks relating to core activity A, then your feedback will show that you are 'proficient'.

On the other hand, if you fail to develop your answers sufficiently, then the feedback will show the following:

Core activity	**Rating**	*You were below the passing standard for this core activity. This is because you did not demonstrate some or all of the following characteristics*
A. Evaluate opportunities to add value	Not proficient	• Demonstrates technical understanding of the models and techniques that are used to add value. • Communicates business recommendations and their justification clearly. • Applies professional judgement in offering advice and recommendations to senior management. • Demonstrates understanding of the business model and its environment, including digital ecosystems and disruptive businesses, and can support senior management in decision making. • Applies professional scepticism to the evaluation of opportunities and the evaluation of proposals. • Demonstrates business awareness in selecting and applying techniques and models with a view to adding value.

The lessons to be learned

Make sure your answer demonstrates the 'soft skills' shown in the final column:

- Have you communicated clearly?
- Have you related your comments to the specific circumstances of the company in the scenario, thus demonstrating 'business awareness' and an 'understanding of the business model'?
- Have you evaluated the extent to which the technique being discussed, such as participation, is useful for the company in the scenario, thus demonstrating 'professional scepticism'?

NB:

It is important that candidates should attempt past cases as part of their preparation and they could ask these three questions with respect to their attempts.

This "critical reflection" will help make the best use of past cases and should develop skills in exam technique.

7 Summary

You should now have a basic understanding of how the case study works. All of the ideas presented in this chapter will be developed further in the remainder of this textbook.

Next steps:

(1) It is a good idea to register with Pearson Vue to see the online version of the Question Tutorial Exam as this will allow you become more familiar with the look and feel of the exam. All the relevant material from the Question Tutorial Exam has been reproduced in this textbook but it is important to recognise that the CIMA case study examinations are dynamic and shouldn't be viewed as equivalent to a static paper exam.

(2) Think about the date on which you will sit the exam and work backwards to create a sensible and achievable study timetable.

(3) You need to ensure that your technical knowledge is up to date / full especially if the OTQ exams were sat a while ago.

It might be worth locating and gathering together any materials you already have from the supporting technical subjects (E2, P2 and F2). We will show you in later chapters how you may need to use these materials.

Chapter

2

Core activities and assessment outcomes

Chapter learning objectives

- To understand the core activities and assessment outcomes required for the case study exam.

1 Core Activities

In some respects one could argue that everything covered in E2, F2 and P2 was still relevant for the Case Study Examination. However, to make such a daunting proposition more accessible and clear, the blueprint defines the following core activities:

	Core Activity	Weighting
A	Evaluate opportunities to add value.	15 – 25%
B	Implement senior management decisions.	15 – 25%
C	Manage performance and costs to aid value creation.	15 – 25%
D	Measure performance.	15 – 25%
E	Manage internal and external stakeholders.	15 – 25%

As stated in chapter 1, **all** core activities will be assessed in each form of the examination in line with the weightings.

These core activities are linked to associated assessment outcomes expressed in terms of 'I Can' statements that speak directly to the skills and competencies that drive the employability of successful learners.

This is seen more clearly when we look at the underlying assessment outcomes below.

2 Assessment outcomes

Assessment outcomes translate core activities into a range of "I can" statements that, in the case study, effectively give you the basis of the wordings for exam tasks.

Given this, it is vital that you look at the assessment outcomes and make sure you feel confident that you could answer a task worded in this way. The full list is as follows:

	Core Activities	Assessment outcomes
A	Evaluate opportunities to add value.	I can select appropriate capital investment appraisal techniques and apply them in order to support capital investment decisions, including product/ service development, digital transformation projects and acquisitions. I can identify and use relevant digital data sources to assist in capital investment decisions. I can explain which pricing strategies are appropriate. I can select and implement suitable business models that will create value for stakeholders, including business models in the context of digital ecosystems. I can analyse the impact of disruptive and digital operating business models in the context of digital ecosystems. I can explain the relevance of weighted average cost of capital
B	Implement senior management decisions.	I can apply appropriate project management tools and techniques to effectively manage projects at the appropriate stage in the project life cycle. I can identify the key project personnel, explain their responsibilities and set appropriate performance measures. I can select and apply suitable tools and techniques for managing risk and uncertainty in capital projects. I can select suitable financing sources and explain the characteristics of the different types of funding. I can recognise the characteristics of high performing teams.

<table>
<tr><td>C</td><td>Manage performance and costs to aid value creation.</td><td>I can advise on the measurement, analysis and reporting on the performance of responsibility centres.
I can analyse the processes needed to ensure employee engagement, empowerment and alignment to enhance individual and team performance.
I can compare leadership styles and identify the most appropriate style to use.
I can use appropriate cost management and cost transformation techniques to manage costs and improve profitability.
I can identify and apply appropriate quality management techniques to enhance value.
I can identify and apply value management techniques to enhance value.
I can apply the techniques that quantify and present risk to stakeholders.</td></tr>
<tr><td>D</td><td>Measure performance</td><td>I can select and apply suitable tools and techniques for managing risk and uncertainty associated with performance related issues.
I can select and apply suitable tools and techniques for managing risk and uncertainty in business models.
I can use the financial statements to assess and report on financial performance and position, interpreting and reporting on a wide range of ratios.
I can support managers by recommending actions to improve financial performance and position and assessing how suggestions impact on the wider organisational ecosystem.
I can select appropriate accounting treatments and explain their implications for users of the financial statements.</td></tr>
<tr><td>E</td><td>Manage internal and external stakeholders.</td><td>I can explain the financial reporting implications of additions to the group.
I can explain the behavioural and transfer pricing issues associated with internal trading.
I can explain the implications of Integrated Reporting for the reporting entity and its stakeholders.
I can advise on the communication process.
I can advise on the negotiation process.
I can advise on conflict management.</td></tr>
</table>

In the next section we will look at how these have been examined in the real exam. Given the syllabus changes in 2019, some tasks in past exams are no longer relevant, so we have focussed on ones that are still indicative of what you might face in your exam.

3 Examples of tasks from the November 2018 exam.

3.1 Summary of pre-seen scenario

To fully appreciate examples from recent real exams it is necessary to have a basic understanding of the case concerned.

The pre-seen information for November 2018 concerns a company called Grapple, one of the major suppliers of soft drinks to the restaurant and retail trade within Zedland.

Grapple is an unlisted entity.

Business model

Founded in 1965 and based in Zedland, Grapple has grown organically since its incorporation, increasing its market share via its reputation for quality and the customer perception that Grapple provides value for money products. In spite of this growth in market share and the increase in Grapple's product range to include carbonated mixers, still mixers and fruit juices, the business continues to be operated from a single site.

Grapple continues to be managed by the original family, currently by Roger Grapple (the son of the founder) who has worked for the business for his entire adult life. Change for Grapple does however seem inevitable as the CEO has expressed a desire to retire in the next five years and none of the descendants seem interested in becoming part of the business.

In addition further change may be necessary as, despite production processes and quality control being strictly monitored, the industry is constantly striving for ways to make its manufacturing processes more efficient and effective due to the pressure on margins. This change may be extremely challenging for Grapple given the longevity of the current leadership.

Competitive position

In the soft drinks sector of the beverages market an industry where market size and brand are key aspects of success, Grapple is still a relatively small player, having only 9% of total market share as of the end of quarter 2 in 2018. It is well worthy of note however that this market share has grown by some 50% when compared against the same period in 2017.

The two main players within the market have a history of significant advertising campaigns which have raised their global profile. This approach to advertising of "pushing" their product to potential customers using emotional and lifestyle attachment is fired by the need to sell high volumes based on their adoption of a "cost leader" approach to strategy; Grapple on the other hand have chosen to adopt a more differentiated approach focussing on quality, product differentiation and innovative recyclable packaging.

Manufacturing process

The manufacturing process of soft drinks, whilst not complex, is sequential in nature with one stage being dependent on another for final product production. Grapple demands the highest level of quality throughout this process which each stage subject to rigorous quality checks. To maintain its status and protect the Grapple brand, Grapple however does depend on external suppliers for its raw materials creating a potential risk.

Industry overview

This highly competitive industry has recently been subject to further challenges from the external environment e.g. those posed by the upsurge in socio-cultural concerns surrounding the sugar content in drinks. The industry is facing significant pressure from social and environmental pressure groups regarding the reduction of sugar content in soft drinks and the associated health issues. This clearly indicates a resultant need for new product development, refinement of packaging and therefore protection of the Grapple brand. These challenges are generating serious risks to the future success of players within the industry and require immediate innovation and action to mitigate the risk.

Information needs

With revenue derived entirely form Zedland is it also essential that Grapple has up to date and accurate information from the market places to facilitate crucial decisions surrounding its product range, distribution channels and market presence. For example, Grapple currently has only 1% of its revenue from airline sales in the central region of Zedland and as a result may consider developing a further presence in this marketplace. This will also be applicable to other overseas expansion opportunities, which is the essence of the original Grapple vision statement.

Future opportunities

All opportunities are fuelled by external pressures and are further complicated by changes in consumer taste, market demand and technological advancement. This requires the need for greater awareness of changes in consumer taste, improvements in technology and social and economic pressures affecting disposable income. This makes for a complex trading environment and a need to understand more about the industry, new production technology and how sales channels are progressing to facilitate decisions concerning Grapple's strategy if growing market share by innovation and product quality and reputation is to be achieved.

Financial performance

The revenue of Grapple increased by 61.0% in 2018 compared to the previous year with operating profit and pre-tax profit increasing by 93.3% and 112.5% respectively indicating very strong growth.

Both the operating profit margin improved from 6.7% in 2017 to 8.1% in 2018, achieved by a combination of revenue growth and control of operating costs. There was similar growth in the pre-tax profit margin over the same period, from 5.4% to 7.1%.

Grapple's return on capital employed improved from 5.9% in 2017 to 10.5% in 2018. A key factor in this was the significant increase in operating profit which almost doubled during this period (Z$6.0m to Z$11.6m).

Financial position

The liquidity position of Grapple appears adequate with a current ratio of 2.6:1 for 2018, albeit with a fall from 3.8:1 in the preceding year. The quick ratio remains healthy, even though it fell from 2.2:1 to 1.7:1 during the same period

It may that these figures disguise an element of inefficiency as there was an increase in both inventories and trade receivables during the period under review. Whilst some increase in inventories and trade receivables may be expected, given the 61% growth in revenue, the increase in inventories and trade receivables was 31.6% and 81% respectively.

Statement of cash flows

Grapple generated a small net increase in cash and cash equivalents for 2018 of Z$0.5m. The key elements from the statement of cash flows are considered below.

Grapple made a profit before tax of Z$10,2m and generated cash from operations of Z$8.7m, which was further reduced to a net cash inflow from operating activities of Z$6.3m after interest and tax payments. Normally a business entity would try to generate a higher net cash inflow of cash from operations as, often, this net inflow would be used to finance net outflows in both investing and financing activities.

Within operating activities, there was a cash outflow resulting from increases in both inventories (Z$6.2m) and trade receivables (Z$20.4m). This cash outflow was offset to some extent by an increase in trade payables of Z$15.3m. Movements in working capital have been considered earlier within this analysis.

The only item within investing activities is a cash outflow of Z$7.0m for payment of PPE, representing 10.8% of the carrying amount of PPE at 30 June 2018.

Within financing activities, there was a small net cash inflow of Z$1.2m, comprising receipt of a loan of Z$6.4m, less payment of a dividend of Z$5.2m. It is noted that the receipt of the loan has, arguably, been used as the source of cash to make the dividend payment.

3.2 Example tasks

In the real exam each task typically covers two core activities. For simplicity we have separated these out to highlight individual assessment outcomes.

Answers are given at the back of the chapter.

A Evaluate opportunities to add value

November 2018 – Variant 4 – Task 2

I can explain which pricing strategies are appropriate

[Trigger and task]

You receive the following email

From: David Guy, Finance Director

To: Finance Manager

Subject: Grapple Sport (confidential) Hi

It looks likely that production will start on the new sports drink, Grapple Sport in the next six months. Roger Grapple's son, Jack, is a majority shareholder and Managing Director of "Jacks" a chain of private gyms across Zedland and has agreed to promote Grapple Sport by selling it in the gyms' cafes. This order will make up 15% of the first year's budgeted sales, which is great news. He is keen to negotiate a special deal so that he can convince his purchasing manager to switch from their current suppliers. He suggests we give him a 15% discount.

Roger thinks this sounds like a good idea and has the backing of the other board members. I think this will need to be stated in Grapple's financial statements for the year ended 30 June 2019. Please let me know whether you agree with me and, if so, what needs to be included in the year end accounts, before I go back to the board? I would like to suggest that we charge the full price with no discount, as I think that will avoid any implications for the financial statements.

The subject of pricing also came up. It was a lively debate with various Board members offering different views. It will be discussed further at the next meeting and for that I would like you to prepare some notes for me to circulate to the Board. Please discuss the suitability of each of the four following suggestions for pricing Grapple Sport when it is launched on the open market and your recommendation.

The suggestions were:

- Discount pricing
- Absorption cost plus 20%
- Penetration pricing
- Price skimming

Thank you

David

Exercise 1

Reply to David's email.

November 2018 – Variant 5 – Task 1

I can explain the relevance of weighted average cost of capital

[Trigger and task]

David Guy calls you into a meeting

"Thanks for coming. I know you are busy with the monthly management information but I'm under pressure from the board to look into funding. Roger told the board at last month's meeting that he would like to retire in three years' time and it's no secret that none of his family are interested in taking over the company. The business has shown significant growth recently and we'd like to capitalise on that, so we are looking at floating Grapple on the Zedland stock exchange. Not only does this give Roger an exit route but it will also provide some funds that will be used for some exciting new projects in the future.

We are confident that if we set a sensible price we will issue sufficient new shares to upgrade the pressing machines in the fruit juice production line leaving 2$30 million for other investment opportunities. The board is considering four projects. I have prepared a spreadsheet showing the amount needed for each, the estimated net present value based on our existing weighted average cost of capital (WACC) of 8% and the profitability index (PI).

Unfortunately, the total investment is more than Z$30m and I think I should have used a revised figure for WACC but did not have time to do this. None of the projects are mutually exclusive.

Taking all of the above into account, I need you to do two things for me:

Secondly, explain whether WACC would remain at 8% now that there are more shares in issue. I'm also wondering whether I should use the cost of equity rather than WACC to appraise this project now that we are funding it through a share issue. Please let me know what you think.

Thanks

David

Exercise 2

Provide your response to David's requests.

[Reference materials]

Projects:

1 Upgrading the bottling plant to include a new facility to use recycled Grapple bottles;

2 Implementation of integrated information system, including new big data management and analytics system for the marketing department;

3 Build a visitor and education centre; 'The Grapple Experience' to raise brand awareness; and

4 Introduce a 'Cycle to Work' scheme and build an onsite gym.

Project number	Investment	Net present value	Profitability index
	Z$m	Z$m	
1	21	5.6	0.27
2	14	3.0	0.21
3	12	3.0	0.25
4	1	(0.4)	(0.4)

B Implement senior management decisions

November 2018 – Variant 5 – Task 2

I can apply appropriate project management tools and techniques to effectively manage projects at the appropriate stage in the project life cycle.

Introduction:

Some months later, the listing of Grapple is well under way. Although the final value available for investment is not yet fully known, it has been decided to go ahead with planning the integrated information system and big data project, with a great focus on the implementation of a new management and analytics system for the marketing department. This has been driven largely by Li Ying, who will act as the project manager for the project.

You have received the following email:

[Trigger and task]

From: Li Ying, Sales and Marketing Director

To: Finance Manager

Subject: big data

I am excited to project manage the proposed big data sub-project, within the larger information system project. As you know this will involve intense collection of data from many sources, including social media. Each time a Grapple product is scanned, either at a distribution centre, or at a retail outlet, we will receive the information accessible at the point of scanning. Every time a social media post mentions one of ours or our competitors' products, we will capture and store that information. This is just the tip of the iceberg. It is a huge, ongoing project which should bring great benefits.

I am familiar with the technology required for a big data system but have no experience in project management. Therefore, I need you to provide some guidance on the stages of this project and what I should consider during each of them.

Li Ying

Exercise 3
Reply to Li Ying's email in the box below

C Manage performance and costs to aid value creation

November 2018 – Variant 3 – Task 3

I can identify and apply appropriate quality management techniques to enhance value

Introduction:

As you are walking through the production area a few days later, Matthew Jones sees you and calls you into his office.

[Trigger and task]

"I've been asked to look into Total Quality Management (TOM)lo try to ensure that issues such as the contamination problem don't happen again. I spoke with David Guy but I didn't like to admit I wasn't sure what he was talking about, so I'm looking for some help. He said there were four different types of costs associated with quality and that introducing TOM should reduce some costs but increase others. I just didn't understand how this could be beneficial.

Please explain TOM and its effect upon the costs of quality. It would be really helpful if you could use our current situation, regarding contamination, to help explain this. I've got some detail of h o w much we have already paid, or have allowed for quality this year if that helps".

[Reference materials]

Actual quality costs Year Ending 30June 2018 (note 1)

	Z$
Quality Control Staff – Salaries and associated costs (note 2)	100,000
Scrapping of finished product due to quality issues	1,550,000
Cleaning and maintenance of equipment	70,000
Training of production staff (note 3)	10,000
Product recall and compensation payments (note 4)	4,500,000

Notes:

1 These are extracts from the management accounts for 2018, following adjustments for the contamination.

2 The quality control officer, Jan Smit, and his team are mainly employed to inspect the products at different stages in the process. They carry out equipment checks once a year and at any other time where the equipment may have been affected by an action such as cleaning.

3 I'm not sure why this is included but I know it's always been reported as a quality cost, since I took over this role

4 Its not normally this high. This is nearly all to do with the contamination

Exercise 4

Draft the responses requested by Matthew.

D Measure performance.

I can select and apply suitable tools and techniques for managing risk and uncertainty in business models.

<u>**November 2018 – Variant 4 – Task 1**</u>

Introduction:

You have been invited to a working party meeting to continue discussions regarding the launch of a new product, Grapple Sport. You were on leave when the last meeting took place and David Guy has just realised he didn't pass the minutes of the previous meeting on to you.

[Trigger and task]

The next meeting is in an hour's time and you will need to provide responses to points raised at the previous meeting. An extract of the minutes from the previous meeting is shown below

Extract of minutes from product launch working party meeting:

Discussion Point	Action
The Finance Director stated that we must not forget the business risks associated with the launch of **a new** product.	For clarification, the Finance Manager was tasked to document the key business risks associated with the product launch and development.

Exercise 5

Provide your response

E Manage internal and external stakeholders

I can explain the behavioural and transfer pricing issues associated with internal trading

November 2018 – Variant 2 – Task 3

Introduction:

Some months later you receive the following email:

[Trigger and task]

From: David Guy, Finance Director

To: Finance Manager

Subject: Issue of transfer pricing

Hi

Having formed a productive joint venture, Fizzcap (formerly referred to as Company X), we need to consider the issue of transfer pricing.

Each of Grapple's production lines will need to purchase bottle caps from the joint venture. I am unwilling to dictate a transfer price, preferring a negotiated approach to setting the price. I would like the teams to sort this out for themselves.

Firstly, I'd like you to briefly explain, to all parties involved, the disadvantages of using the market-based and cost-based approaches towards transfer pricing, and the advantages of using a negotiated approach towards transfer pricing.

Secondly, please also explain the negotiation process to be followed to achieve a positive outcome, providing some detail of how it could be applied.

Thanks

David

Exercise 6

Reply to David's email

I can advise on conflict management

November 2018 – Variant 4 – Task 4

Introduction:

The first year-end bonuses, since Grapple Sport was introduced, have been announced. David Guy calls you in for an urgent meeting to discuss these

[Trigger and task]

"As you know, we did a special deal with Jacks, which allowed it to purchase Grapple Sport at a discounted price. The purchasing for Jacks is carried out by its central procurement team, which is based in our Northern sales area. The Northern Sales Manager has queried his bonus for the year, stating that the special deal has disadvantaged him. He says he usually gets much higher bonuses than the other sales managers, which I checked, and he is correct. Here are this year's calculations for you to have a look at. Please give this some consideration and determine whether there is any justification to his remarks. A general overview of a fair performance measurement system should be included in your response.

Regardless of whether you think he is correct, this has led to conflict, both between him and Li Ying in Sales and Marketing, who he believes is responsible for the decision, and between him and the other sales managers. Keep this to yourself, but I suspect they may have been teasing him about it; you know how competitive they are with each other. Anyway, I don't want the conflict to start to affect working relations irreparably, so I need you to provide me with some suggestions on how to deal with it."

[Reference materials]

Grapple 2019 year- end bonus calculations for regional sales managers

Regional Sales Manager	**Central**	**Northern**	**Southern**
Bonus Calculation (note 1)	Z$	Z$	Z$
Bonus on repeat business	380	420	375
Bonus on new clients (note 2)	1,200	400	1,400
Total Bonus (note 3)	1,580	820	1,775

Notes:

1 All bonuses are based on a combination of a manager's revenue and operating profit margins based on actual results.

2 The total bonus is heavily weighted towards new business, recognising the effort which goes into obtaining new clients. In 2019, the bonus on Grapple Sport was quadruple that of other new business to encourage sales managers to focus on its launch.

3 The Northern Sales Manager received no bonus for Grapple Sport, as the average operating margin for this product in his region was not high enough to reach the minimum threshold for bonuses. 80% of sales of Grapple Sport in his region were to Jacks

Exercise 7
Reply to David's request

4 Summary

Next steps:

(1) You can begin to revisit and revise technical material from your previous studies according to the core activities and assessment outcomes given in this chapter. However we suggest you continue to do this alongside working through the rest of this book so you can also learn how you may need to apply the knowledge.

(2) Remember that you are unlikely to have to perform calculations in the case study exam. However you may need to explain or interpret calculations and so an appreciation of how they are prepared is still relevant and useful.

(3) In the following chapters we do a complete walkthrough of the prototype sample paper issued in June 2019.

5 Solutions to chapter exercises

Exercise 1 – (November 2018 – Variant 4 – Task 2)

Tutorial note:

This question is best answered using the structure provided in the task. It lists four pricing mechanisms for comment and so it does make sense to use that as a structure.

Candidates often waste a lot of time by listing and describing every pricing mechanism that there is before explaining which is relevant.

The key to success is to explain what each method entails and then apply to Grapple. This application of each method will, by definition, "discuss the suitability" of each to Grapple.

Pricing

If we ignore the mathematical approach to pricing, as you suggest, there are two alternative ways of considering how to price Grapple Sport. Strategies may have a differentiation focus or cost focus.

Cost plus % margin

This method of pricing Grapple Sport would involve calculating the production cost and adding, say, 20% of that cost to arrive at the suggested selling price. As you have suggested total absorption costing this will include the unit cost of raw materials, direct labour and variable overheads and a proportion of the fixed costs. This method is easy to calculate for us as we will have the costing information to hand from internal reports. It will also ensure that every unit sold at that price makes Grapple a profit.

However, it has its drawbacks. If the % added is too high, it may make the product much more expensive than those of our competitors. Our customers may not buy our product at that price, so we will not make sufficient profits to cover the costs of production. This could lead to substantial losses for Grapple.

A new product will involve research and development expenditure as well as advertising and marketing costs on the initial launch. We would need to make sure these are covered but if we charged them in the first year it would make the price even higher.

I do not think this would be a suitable method.

Discount pricing

This method would price Grapple Sport much lower than our competitors' sports drinks. Grapple would hope to gain market share and sell in such volume that the total contribution would cover the fixed costs and we would make substantial profits. We would need to make sure that we have demand to sell large volumes. We know that the quality is high but some customers may believe that our prices are lower because the product is inferior to that of our competitors and this may have an effect on our brand value. This may be suitable if the barriers to entry are low, but a large investment is needed in the equipment and research, so I do not think this is suitable.

Penetration Pricing

This method of pricing involves setting a low price on the launch of Grapple Sport and then increasing the price as our customers become more loyal to the product. This is suitable where there are other competitors in the market with products similar to ours and we want to gain market share. We need to make sure that the price is not so low that it is difficult to bring it up to a market price at a later date.

I think this is a suitable method as we have some competition.

Skimming

This method would maximise revenue as it involves setting a high price initially and then lowering it later as other competitors move into the market. It would be the best one in terms of making a return on Grapple Sport. However, the price of this product is unlikely to be inelastic and we may not appeal to a sufficiently large number of customers who are willing to pay this price. The product would need to be unique and highly desirable. We have too many other competitors for this to be the case.

I would not recommend skimming as a suitable pricing strategy.

In conclusion, I would recommend penetration pricing.

Examiners comments

In requirement two, as the pricing headings were provided to the candidates, they found this straightforward as most could give a basic definition of each of them. Most candidates found it difficult to provide anything other than a very basic definition of each of the strategies which limited the marks.

Most candidates did not discuss the suitability of each of the four pricing suggestions. Many only gave an overall conclusion and picked one strategy. That choice was often price skimming as they felt that Grapple's quality product could achieve a high price without appreciating that this was not really an industry suited to price skimming. Marks were also poor for this requirement.

Exercise 2 – (November 2018 – Variant 5 – Task 1)

Tutorial note:

There are two aspects to the requirement:

Explain whether WACC will be affected by an increase in the number of shares *and* whether the project should be evaluated at the cost of equity or WACC.

The question is seeking an understanding of cost of equity and WACC. How will changing the weighting of equity to debt affect WACC? Which of the two figures is the more relevant to this appraisal exercise?

Candidates are reminded to stick closely to the requirement.

WACC

There are two questions to answer here:

1 Will WACC change if there is a new issue of shares; and

2 Should Grapple be using WACC as a discount factor to appraise projects or should we be using the cost of equity.

Will WACC change?

WACC is calculated as an average cost of Grapple's finance (debt and equity) weighted according to the proportion of each element in the pool of funds. These weightings are based on the market values of the debt and equity. The cost of equity of Grapple is higher than the cost of debt. It therefore follows that WACC will increase if there is more equity in the capital structure. It will be above 8% and using this as a discount factor would cause the net present values of each project to reduce.

Should the cost of equity be used?

Grapple should not use the cost of equity just because the new project is being funded from equity. The new funds are being put into the pool of funds and Grapple is using all funding to operate the business. It is appropriate to use WACC.

Further reasons would include:

1. It assumes that the level of gearing (the proportion of debt to equity) will remain unchanged for the foreseeable future. Grapple has not suggested that further finance will be issued or whether they wish to change the balance of debt to equity.
2. The projects to be undertaken do not change the business risk of Grapple I.e. they do not take Grapple into a different line of activity.
3. These new projects seem to be substantial and not insignificant to Grapple.

Examiners comments

The second requirement of the first section was weak. Some candidates were aware that equity would be more expensive than debt so WACC would increase as more equity is being issued and that it therefore made more sense to recalculate WACC post flotation and with the particular large projects in mind. On the whole, most candidates offered very limited answers for this half of the question beyond WACC being a better measure, usually stated simply and without reasons.

Exercise 3 – (November 2018 – Variant 5 – Task 2)

Tutorial note:

It is essential to be sure that you have understood and therefore answered the requirement in the task. In this task it is not about *"big data"* but the fact that Li has *"no experience in project management. Therefore, I need you to provide some guidance on the stages of this project"*. The key is use each of the stages of a project and then apply to them to the circumstances in the "trigger" and "pre-seen" information.

Stages of Project Management

Whilst different models of project management suggest slightly different stages, the activities within them remain similar. It is worth noting that some of the stages may be carried out in conjunction with other sub-projects of this overall information systems project. This answer, however, treats it as a stand-alone project. Taking a simple five- stage approach to project management, the stages would be as follows:

Initiation – This appears to have been mainly completed, given that the Board have already approved the project, and carried out a cost-benefit analysis. The purpose of the stage is to determine whether or not to actually go ahead with a project, culminating in the production of a Project Initiation Document (PID). The activities which should have already been completed would be a business case, justifying the project, and an overview of the objectives and the risks involved.

It would seem that the risk management has not yet been completed, but this is sometimes considered in the planning stage, and I would certainly recommend that takes place to minimise any potential impact on the project or its outcomes.

The PID, if it has not already been produced, should include the objectives, scope, timeline and basic budget for the project. For example, the scope seems to suggest that the Big Data system will be for marketing only, so this project may not capture the data for other purposes.

Planning – This should include a comprehensive plan of all aspects of the project before the initiation actually takes place. An important element will be the work breakdown structure and network diagram, which will allow for the planning of individual activities such that the project can be completed in the most time-effective way possible. It will be necessary to determine dependencies such that there is no time wasted during the project. For example, it will be necessary to purchase the data storage hardware and software and install it, prior to beginning the data collection activities. Other elements of planning include the quality plan; again, this will be of vital importance. The quality of the project and its deliverables could influence whether we are in breach of data protection regulations. There should also be human resource planning, procurement planning, communications planning and budgeting taking place during this stage. Finally, there should be a plan for measurement of success, such that it will be possible to determine, post-completion, whether the project has been a success or not.

Implementation – This stage is where the project appears to get fully underway. The plans can be put into place. This will include the actual purchasing and installation of the hardware and software, as well as the training of staff and the design of the data collection, storage and analysis techniques.

Monitoring and Control – This stage usually takes place simultaneously with the implementation stage. The project manager should use exception reports to ascertain whether the project is on track. These can cover all the major constraints such as time, cost and scope. Projects should have defined gateways at which there are deliverables to be signed off by the project manager and any required stakeholders e.g. there could be a gateway when all hardware has been installed, requiring sign off by the project manager and the procurement and installation teams. Anything going off track should be recognised immediately and dealt with accordingly.

Completion – This stage comprises three key aspects; the closing of the project, the post-project review and the benefits review. The closing of the project is mainly administrative, ensuring all documentation has been completed, all deliverables are in place and all suppliers have been paid.

The post-project review usually takes place a few months after completing the implementation stage and considers what went well or badly in the project itself. This could include whether it was completed on time, to budget, and included only the defined scope. It could also consider softer aspects such as how well-managed the project was and whether the team worked well together.

Finally, the post-completion or benefits review would take place some months or sometimes even years after the project ends; sufficient time to see whether the listed benefits have been met. I have not seen the listed benefits for this particular project, but I assume there will be some specific sales growth targets or increase in brand recognition for example. It will be important to have sufficient data to measure these.

It is at this final stage where any unintended benefits recognised will be discussed, as well as potential for future projects related to this one, perhaps, in this case, to extend the projected use of the system.

Examiners comments

Requirement one was about project management, however the question caused the candidates difficulty as they did not seem to understand what was required. Candidates seemed unsure whether they should be answering specifically with the Big Data implementation project in mind.

Some good scripts gave good structured coverage to project management stages covering the complete lifecycle and indicating the necessary access to skills within the PM team. However most simply wrote everything they knew relating to project management, often without structure or demonstrating any understanding of purpose or the grouping of activities under the stages. This did not gain high marks.

Exercise 4 – November 2018 – Variant 3 – Task 3

Tutorial note:

As in the previous exercise, it is essential to be sure that you have understood the requirement in the task, before answering the question. In this task you are required to "*please explain TQM and its effect upon the costs of quality. It would be really helpful if you could use our current situation, regarding contamination to help explain this*".

The key is therefore to make clear what TQM is, the effect on costs of quality (explain) and then apply this knowledge to the circumstances in the "trigger" and "pre-seen" information, In this instance the situation regarding contamination.

Total quality Management and the costs of quality

Total Quality Management (TQM) is an organisational approach which aims to get things 'right first time' across the entire business. However, just because things are done correctly, it doesn't mean they can't improve, so there is also a focus on continual improvement. For example, getting it right first time would mean introducing policies and procedures to ensure that errors such as the recent contamination would not happen again. However, continuous improvement might also include a change in the cleaning process so it is more efficient and effective.

There are four basic categories of quality costs, divided into two types; costs of compliance and costs of failure, as follows:

Cost of compliance	Costs of failure
Prevention costs	Internal failure costs
Appraisal costs	External failure costs

Prevention costs are those costs incurred in trying to prevent any quality failures; such as the training of production staff and the cleaning and maintenance of equipment, which you have stated come to Z$80,000 when combined.

Appraisal costs would include all inspection costs, which seem to be the main use of quality control staff from note 2, and so would be Z$100,000 in your accounts.

Internal failure costs are the costs of correcting any issues before they reach the customer or an external party. So, if your quality control team found an error, it would be the cost of dealing with this, either scrapping the product or re-working it. You have recognised Z$1,550,000 for scrapping of liquid, which would be categorised as an internal failure cost.

Finally, and this is the least desirable expense, is the *external failure* cost of Z$4,500,000. This is the cost of dealing with any quality issues which have already affected the external environment or especially, the customer. If there is an expense in this category, it suggests that all other stages failed. This is the case with the recent contamination, and as you can see, can be very expensive to rectify.

TQM should be across the organisation and includes shared ownership. It seems, at the moment, that quality is seen as a production issue only. However, it would be necessary to have procedures in place in purchasing for example. Purchasing staff should be involved in a quality circle with production for example. Grapple is a drinks producer and therefore the external costs may be high especially for financial and reputational impacts.

With the 'right first time' ethos of TQM, prevention costs should see an increase as there would be a lot of activity towards preventing failure e.g. quality circles to discuss each business area, creation of policies and procedures to ensure good quality and training of staff. However, this should have a positive effect on the other costs of quality. If we do get it right, there should be no costs of failure at all. As costs of failure are usually disproportionate to what the costs would be to prevent failure, this should have a positive effect on the total costs of quality.

Over time, as the TQM initiative proves successful, it is also possible to reduce the costs of checking, as, if you have all the processes in place to 'get it right' then the checking becomes redundant. Given that our product is a food type, however, there will always be some mandatory quality checks.

Examiners comments

The first requirement asked for an explanation of TQM and whether it might be beneficial for the company. Most candidates were able to offer clear explanations of TQM and to list the different costs of quality. Candidates were generally weaker on the question of whether TQM would be beneficial in this case. Generally, application consisted of classifying the costs listed in the reference materials in terms of the descriptive headings offered in response to the first part of the requirement.

Exercise 5 – (November 2018 – Variant 4 – Task 1)

Tutorial note:

In this task you are asked to *"document the key business risks associated with the product launch and development"*. It is critical therefore to note that the product in question is "new" and reflect this in your response. Any risk will score good marks only if it is applicable to the content in the trigger and the pre-seen material.

The response can be well structured by using each identified risk as a separate subheading, briefly explain "what" the risk is and justifying "why" it is relevant.

Business Risks associated with product development

Business risks can be considered to cover a number of different categories.

The key ones associated with product launch may be considered to be as follows:

Strategic risk – This is the risk that a new strategy, in this case a new product, will fail. However, if managed correctly, it should not affect our overall strategy, which should remain positive, as it currently is. This is exemplified by our exceptional growth rates due to our existing products.

Product risk – This includes both the risk of the failure of the new product itself, which would be costly to us e.g. as a result of development, production and marketing costs, which may not be recovered. There is also the risk to our existing products i.e. if Grapple Sport is bought by customers as a replacement to existing drinks. This seems unlikely, as it will be designed to meet a very different purpose.

Reputational risk – As mentioned previously, there is a risk that our brand image, and reputation, may be affected if we choose the wrong strategy for our product launch. Given our awareness of this, we should ensure that we manage the launch so as to avoid this, but we should consider all eventualities, such as potential health issues associated with drinks or if it contains too much sugar for a sports drink for example, given the recent focus on this.

Operational risk – There is the risk that the processes we implement to produce this new product may fail. We will need to ensure that this is well-planned. Taking into consideration that we already produce a variety of drinks, it is unlikely that we will fail in this area unless we use entirely new methods and equipment.

Examiners comments

In requirement 3, many candidates could list business risks and this was answered fairly well with risks such as customers not liking the taste, possible sugar tax issues, competition beating them to the launch, production/capacity issues all being fairly common.

What candidates didn't do very well was to evaluate the risks. This may be as it wasn't specifically asked for, sometimes candidates discussed how the risks could be mitigated, but they didn't usually do this for all the risks identified. Some just listed TARA and gave theory without applying it to the scenario at all.

Exercise 6 – (November 2018 – Variant 2 – Task 3)

Tutorial note:

You are tasked to *"briefly explain to all parties involved the disadvantages of using the market-based and cost-based approaches towards transfer pricing, and the advantages of using a negotiated approach towards transfer pricing"*; and secondly *"explain the negotiation process to be followed to achieve a positive outcome, providing some detail of how it could be applied"*.

The response can be well structured by using each identified sub-task as a separate subheading. From there briefly explain "what" each aspect of transfer pricing requested is and the advantages and disadvantages of each to Grapple.

The second part can be more difficult and it would be easy for the response to drift away from that which is required. Syllabus knowledge is critical here to provide a clear structure for your response e.g. the four stages of negotiation i.e. preparation, opening, bargaining and closing and then applying these to the circumstances of accepting transfer pricing principles.

It is not nearly enough however to just identify these four stages.

The response should apply negotiation skills in context of the preseen information and "trigger". The examiner is looking for an appreciation of the issues arising from the discussion within Grapple, e.g. the implications of being unable to reach a mutually satisfactory agreement.

Transfer Pricing

Generally, transfer prices should be acceptable to both the receiving and supplying parties. The use of transfer pricing should also benefit the organisation as a whole, in this case potentially restricting supplies to Grapple's competitors and causing them to pay higher prices elsewhere.

A good transfer pricing system should be adopted which does not encourage either party to buy or sell the product in question on the open market. This is less likely at the moment as the particular type of bottle top has only been seen at overseas trade fairs, but if we start producing it, it is only a matter of time before there are local competitors.

One of the disadvantages of market-based transfer pricing is that the purchasing department obtains little benefit, even if the organisation does as a whole. The market price might be quite high, as high prices are often prevalent in the introduction/growth stages of the product lifecycle, which is where this product currently is. Matching the market price might reduce product margins in our product lines significantly.

The fluctuations of market prices should also be considered as this would make it difficult to budget and lead to fluctuating results.

A cost-based transfer price could take different forms but would usually include the cost (either marginal or full) plus a mark-up for profit.

A key consideration is whether actual or standard costs would be used. Actual costs may fluctuate, leaving the receiving production lines with fluctuating costs and margins themselves.

The main disadvantage with the use of standard costs is that Fizzcap would have no incentive to reduce costs, as it would always meet its desired profit. Additionally, standard costs may be set on historical facts, and may not be changed when production is improved e.g. if there was a learning curve effect, thus disadvantaging the receiving department.

The advantages of using a negotiated approach is that all factors can be considered when setting the price, including the characteristics of the intermediate market and the performance measurement systems affecting both parties. The negotiated approach should allow both parties to feel empowered, which could motivate them towards their goals. It should allow the selling division to make a greater profit if they were able to operate more efficiently, thus encouraging them to reduce costs.

Negotiation

Negotiation is about reaching an agreement, as opposed to one party 'winning' and another 'losing' the discussion. This is particularly true about transfer pricing, as both parties should benefit from this.

The negotiation process involves four stages; preparation, opening, bargaining and closing.

During the *preparation* stage, the production managers should carry out internal and external research. For example, both supplying and receiving parties need to know what the market price is. The supplying party needs to consider its costs and what margin it wishes to achieve. The receiving party should also consider the end price it wishes to charge, and the margin it wishes to achieve.

The *opening* stage requires each party to state its opening position. The supplying party may open with market price, whereas the receiving party is likely to open with a low offer, in order to maximise its profit. As this is a new type of product top, it may be that the opening position of the receiving party is the price paid for the existing bottle tops. However, this may be difficult to match as the technology is new and may incur greater production costs.

Bargaining involves the discussions required to reach a final agreement, at the *closing* stage. This should ensure that both parties benefit, as well as the organisation overall. In this case, Fizzcap should cover its costs in the long run, and the Grapple production lines should not feel disadvantaged e.g. the production managers should not see their performance measurement affected detrimentally.

It is worth noting that the negotiation can be revisited or could specifically allow for changing costs and market conditions over the product lifecycle.

Examiners comments

A good answer here would not only explain the features of a well thought out transfer pricing system but also relate it to the specific scenario presented by the case study. Although this section was generally reasonably well attempted many candidates omitted discussion of the negotiation process. Explaining the four stages of negotiation, preparation, opening, bargaining and closing would have been appropriate.

Exercise 7 – (November 2018 – Variant 4 – Task 4)

Tutorial note:

You are tasked by the FD as follows: *"I don't want the conflict to start to affect working relations irreparably, so I need you to provide me with some suggestions on how to deal with it".* This is in the specific context of a "special" deal with one of Grapples customers to purchase Grapple Sport

It is clear therefore that a brief understanding if the type of conflict displayed would benefit how it could be resolved. The response can be well structured in this context outing the type of conflict and the most appropriate methodology for its resolution.

Syllabus knowledge and its application to the circumstance in the pre-seen and "trigger" are again vital for a good answer.

Conflict resolution

Two types of conflict are evident here; vertical conflict between the Northern Sales Manager and Li Ying and horizontal conflict between him and the other sales managers.

To deal with the horizontal conflict first; this is not always a bad thing if it can become constructive conflict. We know that our sales managers are very competitive with each other and this can be constructive, encouraging them all to improve and perform well against their colleagues. However, it appears the competition may have gone a step too far, in this case, and is in danger of becoming destructive. The other two sales managers may be alienating the Northern Sales Manager. This, combined with the bonus problem, may demotivate him and cause his departure, which we would not want to happen.

I would suggest that conflict resolution or conflict reduction may be appropriate here. A social event may help break the bad atmosphere and allow them to go back to 'business as normal'.

Alternatively, we could encourage the three sales managers to collaborate in order to suggest a new basis for the bonus scheme. This would be seeking a win-win solution and encourage cohesiveness as a group.

Of course, it is possible that they wouldn't all agree, and the conflict couldn't be resolved completely. In this case, conflict reduction would be appropriate. This would involve building on areas of agreement in order to break down barriers and change attitudes about the other parties involved. It may be that there is some jealousy involved if the Northern Sales Manager usually gets better bonuses. If he could explain to the others how he achieves high sales bonuses, they could all share their best practices and all could benefit from this, as well as the company.

The vertical conflict may need gentler handling. Li Ying is the line manager and may consider this insubordinate behaviour towards her. If they are to maintain a professional relationship, it must be resolved quickly.

Simple communication could be the key here. It was not Li Ying's decision to take on the special deal, but that of the entire Board. This could be explained, but I feel it is unlikely to do much to appease things; it might just spread the conflict wider.

It may be that Li Ying chooses to avoid the conflict; that is, either pretend it is not present, and carry on as normal, or discipline the sales manager for unprofessional behaviour. The latter is likely to exacerbate the situation. It is possible that ignoring it could work; sometimes initial conflict is in the heat of the moment and dies down after a while.

Given my earlier suggestion that the bonus scheme should be adapted to eradicate the result of this uncontrollable special deal, it could be that Li Ying, as the bearer of this news, may find the conflict automatically resolves itself. This might be considered to be an accommodating approach to conflict resolution, and seems appropriate in this case. However, there may be an issue in the future if the sales manager feels he can force his manager into accommodating his employment terms and conditions.

Alternatively, as with my suggestion for the sales managers working together to propose a new bonus scheme, Li Ying could also be involved in this, and be seen as a collaborator. She could lead the negotiation in which all parties should benefit, to remove any conflict.

Examiners comments

As for requirement two, candidates did not seem to realise they needed to talk generally about conflicts therefore it was very rare to see any candidates mentioning vertical or horizontal conflicts. Instead they launched straight into resolution.

For the resolution this was usually reasonable as most candidates discussed the need for communication all round, including bringing in HR or one of the directors, and the possibility of increasing the manager's bonus.

This question was not done very well; candidates seemed to be ill prepared in all areas.

6 Examiners comments – common themes

- It is imperative that the candidate answers the task as set. This means fully understanding the task requirement and the verb before writing your response.
- Ensure that answer you prepare links to both the pre-seen scenario and any additional relevant information raised in the "trigger"?
- Ensure that any solutions or recommendations presented are practical and realistic, taking into account the circumstances facing the organisation.
- It is imperative to apply your knowledge rather than just prepare a "brain dump" of facts from the study text.
- Students need to practice actually typing answers to cases and reflecting on what they have written to consider whether it is sufficiently full and correct.
- Exchanging answers with a study partner would give both the opportunity to put them in the marker's position by giving feedback on what they like or dislike about each other's responses.

Chapter

3

2019 prototype exam – pre-seen information

1 Introduction

The Case Study Examinations are like no other CIMA exam; there is no new syllabus to study or formulae to learn. The best way to be successful at this level is to practise using past case study exams and mock exams based on your real live case study. By reviewing previous case studies alongside your current case you will improve your commercial thought processes and will be more aware of what the examiner expects. By sitting mock exams, under timed conditions you can hone your exam techniques and, in particular, your time management skills.

This textbook is therefore based on this principle. It presents the prototype case study and uses this to demonstrate the skills and techniques that you must master to be successful. The prototype case, Grainger, will be used to walkthrough the processes and approach. The remainder of this chapter contains the Grainger pre-seen material.

We would advise that you skim read this now before moving on to Chapter 4 where you will be provided with more guidance on how to familiarise yourself with the pre-seen material.

GRAINGER

Contents

Job description

You are a Financial Manager with Grainger. You report to Janine Frier, a Senior Financial Manager, who in turn reports to the Finance Director.

Your primary responsibilities are associated with management accounting. This means that you often have to liaise with colleagues from the treasury and financial reporting functions and also from other functional areas, including Sales, Human Resources and Operations.

Organisation background

Grainger designs and manufactures mobile phones.

The company is based in Deeland, which is a developed and industrialised country. Deeland requires the application of IFRS for financial reporting. The country's currency is the D$.

Since it was founded in the 1950s to manufacturer consumer electronics, such as radios, Grainger has developed and adapted its product range over the years in response to developments in consumer tastes and trends. By the early 1990s, Grainger was a major manufacturer of mobile phones and by 1998, it was making nothing but mobile phones. Grainger is a global manufacturer and its products can be purchased in most countries around the world.

Grainger was quoted on the Deeland stock exchange in 1999.

Mobile network infrastructure

Mobile phones themselves would be useless without the extensive infrastructure created by the network providers that make it possible for the phones to make or receive calls from almost any populated area on Earth.

The infrastructure is based on relatively low-powered radio base stations that have adjoining or overlapping coverage, so that a phone user is always within range of at least one base station.

The base stations can be free standing, or mounted on top of buildings. In cities, there are often small systems mounted on the sides of buildings. The base stations have a relatively short range and so establishing a mobile phone network is a complicated and expensive undertaking, in order to ensure that population centres are covered. It is also necessary to build and operate base stations alongside motorways and other major roads.

Mobile network providers

Mobile phone manufacturers such as Grainger do not provide the phone services or infrastructure. Most countries have several network providers who compete to sell connections to phone users. Users pay to use these services in two ways: 'pay monthly' and 'pay as you go'.

Under a pay monthly contract, the customer pays the mobile network provider at the end of each month for calls made and other services that have been used. There is usually a fixed element to the monthly payment, which covers access to the network and also some calls and other services. There will be an additional variable element to the payment if the customer uses additional call time or other services. The network provider has the customer's bank details and collects monthly payments by direct debit.

Pay monthly contracts are typically for two years. The network providers usually give the customer a phone as an incentive to sign the contract and a replacement (or 'upgrade') phone when the user renews at the contract's end. Those phones will either be 'free' or will require the customer to pay a heavily discounted price that is usually 20-25% of the phone's retail value. The networks are effectively selling these phones on credit because they recoup their costs by building a repayment into the fixed element of the monthly fee.

Pay monthly customers are effectively being sold new mobile phones every two years, whenever they renew their contracts. As an incentive to attract or retain customers, the network providers use their buying power to obtain discounts when they buy phones and they pass much of that discount onto their customers.

A pay as you go customer must pay in advance to use the mobile network. Advance payments can be made by buying a voucher from a shop, by making a card payment or by using some bank automated teller machines (ATMs). The resulting credit is tracked by the network providers' systems and is used whenever the phone makes a call or accesses another service.

The network providers ensure that pay as you go phones are sold at a discount to their full retail value, again as an incentive to attract customers. That discount is less generous for a pay as you go phone than for pay monthly because a customer who buys a pay as you go phone is under no legal obligation to buy further credit.

Sim cards

Each mobile phone is identified by a SIM card, which carries unique identifying data. The network provider issues the SIM card to the user. Changing the SIM card changes the identity of the phone, including its phone number.

All phone manufacturers, including Grainger, generally 'lock' their phones by entering an encrypted setting in the phone's operating system. A locked phone will work only with a SIM card issued by a designated network provider, thereby forcing the phone's owner to use that network provider's service. Locking the phone protects the network provider, who has given the customer a discount from the retail price. Otherwise, customers could buy their phones from one network and insert SIM cards from another.

It is possible to buy unlocked phones, which will work with any network. The lack of a discount from the network supplier makes them expensive to buy.

Network providers often have their own retail channels to sell phones and SIM cards. These can include both shops and online sales. These channels carry the network provider's brand. They sell pay monthly and pay as you go phones, with associated service contracts, that are locked to their own networks.

Mobile phones can also be purchased from independent retailers, who generally sell phones on behalf of a variety of network providers. Network providers give the retailers commissions so that the customer pays the same for a pay monthly contract or a pay as you go phone obtained through a retailer or through the network provider.

Although Grainger's business model does not include selling mobile phone's directly to the phone user, it does have a direct relationship with the users.

In order for users to take advantage of Grainger's standard manufacturer's warranty for their phone, they are required to register their details online on Grainger's website. This also allows the users to receive advance information about new phone models that are in development, as well as to access the online support forum.

This involves the user registering their email address to create an account which is password protected. Full name and address details are also required to be provided as part of the registration process.

Users can also take up the option of an extended warranty on their phone. The cost of this depends upon the length of time they wish to take the extended warranty out for and whether they also want to include accidental damage cover. Payment for this is taken by credit card.

Mobile phones and their uses

When mobile phones were first developed, their primary function was to enable users to make and receive phone calls when they were away from home. Over time, various functions have been added and voice calls have become increasingly irrelevant to many users. For example, SMS text messaging rapidly gained popularity and it became commonplace to communicate by text message in place of making voice calls.

The function of mobile phones is constantly being redefined, thanks to the flexibility associated with the underlying technology. A mobile phone is essentially a handheld computer that incorporates radio facilities for wireless communication. In addition to the wireless connection to the mobile phone network, most phones have the ability to connect directly to wireless local area networks through Wi-Fi and to other nearby electronic devices through Bluetooth.

Mobile phones are frequently used to access the internet and email and are frequently used to update social media accounts and to engage in online commerce.

Many phones come equipped with cameras. Many users rely on their camera phones for their photographic needs, to the point where phone cameras are rivalling basic digital cameras in terms of quality. Camera sales are declining because of improvements in phone cameras.

Phones are also used as personal music players and handheld games consoles, again displacing audio players and portable games devices.

It is becoming increasingly common for householders to dispense with traditional landlines for making phone calls. Landlines are often used for internet access and mobile phones are used for all voice calls.

Quite apart from the technical developments, many users regard their phones as fashion accessories. Perfectly functional phones are often replaced in order to remain abreast of current trends. So-called 'smartphones' offer the level of functionality described above, although there is also a market for basic mobile phones that may be used by those who find smartphones too complicated or who need an inexpensive phone to allow, say, a child to stay in contact when away from home.

Most manufacturers, including Grainger, concentrate their development efforts on their smartphones. Upgrades to existing models are often incremental, for example a slightly better camera or a slimmer, more lightweight or attractive case.

Software issues

All electronic devices, including mobile phones, rely on operating systems to enable the hardware to function.

In the early days of mobile phones, each manufacturer developed a basic operating system to translate, say, key presses into electronic instructions such as accepting an incoming call.

Over time, mobile phones have become increasingly complicated to the point where it would be uneconomic to develop separate operating systems. Most manufacturers use an open source operating system that has been adapted slightly to meet their specific needs. Open source means that the operating system's owner grants permission to install it free of charge and to adapt it as required. For example, Grainger's smartphones display the company's logo when the phone is being powered up and the various screens that the users interact with were all designed by Grainger.

Users can also buy software applications (known as 'apps') that enable them to add functions to their phones. A wide range of apps is available, ranging from games to business software such as word processors. Some apps are free to download and use and others must be paid for. Many electronics companies release apps that enable the user's mobile phone to operate as remote controls for their products. For example, some televisions can be operated using apps running on compatible phones. Apps may have also have specialised uses, such as assisting pilots to prepare and file flight plans.

Grainger's use of the open source operating system that has become the industry-standard is very much a mixed blessing. On the plus side, it means that it need not incur the costs associated with developing and updating its own operating system. The operating system's owner does not charge for its use. Potential buyers know that they will be able to install a wide selection of apps. The operating system can also exchange files with their laptops and tablets. On the downside, most of Grainger's direct competitors use the same operating system, which gives their phones a similar appearance to Grainger's.

Radio frequencies and data connections

Radio communications work by transmitting a signal that is pitched at a specific frequency. The signal can then be captured using a receiver that is set to the same frequency. That principle is true for all forms of wireless communications, including radio and television broadcasts, radio communications by the military and emergency services, and other telecommunications, including mobile phones. Most countries have very strict laws governing radio transmissions, otherwise there would be a risk of interference between signals. Most governments treat radio frequencies as a national resource. Over the years there have been four generations of mobile phone, each of which has occupied a different area of the radio frequency spectrum. The changes have arisen because the laws of physics mean that some frequencies are more suitable than others for communications. Moving mobile phones to different frequency bands can also reduce the risk of interference between mobile phone communications and other services.

New generations of mobile phone occupy different frequencies and they require the network providers to install new base technologies. The overall effect has generally been to increase network capacity, meaning that mobile phone networks are unlikely to be swamped by the volume of calls. It also means that data can be transferred more quickly and the quality of voice communication has improved. The volume of data that can be carried over any given channel is often referred to as 'bandwidth'.

Mobile phone generations

Each generation of mobile phone has been numbered. Today, most mobile phones operate as either 3G or 4G. 3G remains in widespread use around the world and offers features such as basic internet browsing, receiving and transmitting data files (such as photographs). 4G phones are faster still in comparison to 3G, and 4G networks are now generally available. Phones are generally 'backwards compatible' which means that they can use older networks when required. So, a 4G phone that is out of range of a 4G network can connect to any available 3G or 2G network, albeit at the slower speeds specified by those earlier generations.

Latest developments

5G is the name given to the latest generation of wireless networks. The relevant standards are still in the process of being defined. The ambiguity around 5G is because it's still largely a concept at this point, and the wireless industry hasn't settled on any standards around the new network. Some key goals of 5G include:

- Significantly faster data speeds: Currently, 4G networks are capable of achieving peak download speeds of one gigabit per second (Gbps), though in practice it's never that fast. With 5G, this would increase to 10Gbps.
- Ultra-low latency: 'Latency' refers to the time it takes one device to send a packet of data to another device. Currently with 4G, the latency rate is around 0.05 of a second, but 5G will reduce that to about 0.001of a second. This is a significant improvement when data has to be communicated in as close to real time as possible. For example, the precise operation of remote industrial equipment or the safe navigation of driverless cars will benefit from this reduction in latency.
- A more 'connected world': a phenomenon referred to as 'The Internet of Things' involves building connectivity into products and devices such as domestic appliances, cars and even wearable devices. So, if your car develops a fault it could email details to your local garage and enter the service appointment into your online diary. The growth in this technology will cause an exponential growth in the number of devices connected to the internet and will require a network that can accommodate billions of connected devices. Part of the goal behind 5G is to provide that capacity, and also to be able to assign bandwidth depending on the needs of the application and user.

Clearly, 5G offers capabilities that go far beyond enhancing the use of mobile phones. For example, the 5G network would have sufficient bandwidth for household appliances to communicate routinely over the internet. A domestic fridge could have a scanner that reads the barcodes on products as they are purchased and subsequently used. The fridge could then order replenishments from an on-line supermarket or its owner could use an app to check whether there is, say, fresh milk in the fridge before coming home.

Each new generation of phones has created opportunities and challenges for phone manufacturers. Grainger's earliest models were made for 2G. Now the company offers a range of 4G smartphones. Grainger's management team is studying the potential created by 5G, even though it is unlikely to be operational before 2020 and, even then, it is likely to be another two years or more before 5G networks become widely operational across most of the countries in which Grainger operates in. Thus, although work continues on developing a new range of 5G ready smartphones, Grainger's current focus remains on improving the company's range of 4G phones to further exploit the opportunities offered by new and improved versions of the operating systems and the ever-increasing range of smartphone apps that are being developed.

Battery technology

Mobile phones depend on batteries for power. A battery is essentially a pair of electrodes that are connected electrically by a substance called an electrolyte. Chemical reactions between these components create electricity when a circuit is completed between the two electrodes. For example, switching on a mobile phone completes an electrical circuit and electricity flows from the battery until the chemical reaction has finished.

Some batteries are rechargeable, which means that the chemical reaction that created the electricity can be reversed by running an electrical current through the battery. This can be repeated many times, although most batteries deteriorate slightly with each recharging cycle and eventually lose the ability to be recharged.

The potential to create electricity from a rechargeable battery is generally a function of the materials used in its construction and also the size of the battery.

Battery life is a significant aspect of a mobile phone's performance. Whenever a mobile phone is switched on, it makes frequent connections to the network in order to update the network's ability to route calls and other messages to the phone. Calls and messaging consume power, as does any activity that requires the use of the screen because the backlighting that makes the screens LCD panel visible consumes a great deal of power. Battery life is also constrained by trends and tastes in phone styles. Users value slim phones that are easy to carry and that look sleek. Making phones slimmer leaves less internal volume for a large battery.

Mobile phone manufacturers are constantly evaluating the latest battery technology because users are often frustrated by their phones running out of charge. It is not uncommon for users to be forced to recharge their phones every night in order to obtain a full day's use next day.

Rechargeable batteries can create problems for manufacturers and users. They produce a fairly high current and the process of charging and discharging rechargeable batteries can also create a great deal of heat. That can raise safety concerns. For example, fuel stations forbid the use of mobile phones while operating fuel pumps because of the slight risk of a spark created by a rechargeable battery igniting the vapour from the car's fuel tank.

Extract from Grainger's Integrated Report

Our Vision

To be recognised globally as the number one manufacturer of smartphones

Our Mission

To provide high quality products and industry leading levels of customer service, delivered by experienced and empowered staff. We aim to recognise the needs and desires of our stakeholders in all of our operations.

Staff

We recognise that, in order to satisfy the needs of Grainger's other stakeholders, it is vital that we attract and retain the best people. We are committed to providing industry-leading career opportunities for all staff and are proud of our record as an equal opportunity employer, dating back to well before legislation was introduced to ensure such practices were adhered to.

All staff are encouraged to develop a tailored training programme, in agreement with their line manager. We also encourage our staff to engender relationships with the local community and, in addition, provide up to 5 additional paid days annual leave for them to dedicate time to their chosen charitable causes.

We offer a competitive remuneration package that includes above average basic salaries, a profit-related bonus scheme and other incentives such as private health care, generous maternity and paternity leave and staff discounts

Shareholders

Our shareholders range from individual investors to venture capitalists and large institutional investors. However, regardless of the level of shareholding, we are committed to building strong, transparent relationships with all of our investors, through regular shareholder meetings and email communications as well as the dedicated investor section of our corporate website.

We fully recognise that, without the continued support from our shareholders, we would not be able to maintain the growth strategies that we need to pursue in order for us to maintain our competitive advantage and sustainability.

Customers

We aim to always deliver only high quality products and services to our customers. Our staff are thoroughly trained to produce value-adding and defect-free products and exemplary levels of customer service, based on constant feedback obtained from regular customer surveys and day to day interaction with customers.

We are very proud of our record of being amongst the top 3 mobile phone suppliers globally for product quality and customer service, for each of the past 10 years, and our aim is to become the number one supplier every year.

Suppliers

We continue to build relationships with our suppliers and see them very much as part of our organisational ecosystem, along with our other key stakeholders. A reliable supply of quality components is vital if we are to provide products to the standards that our customers have come to expect from us.

We have invested heavily over the past couple of years in a number of joint projects with several of our suppliers, resulting in mutually beneficial outcomes for all parties.

Management Structure

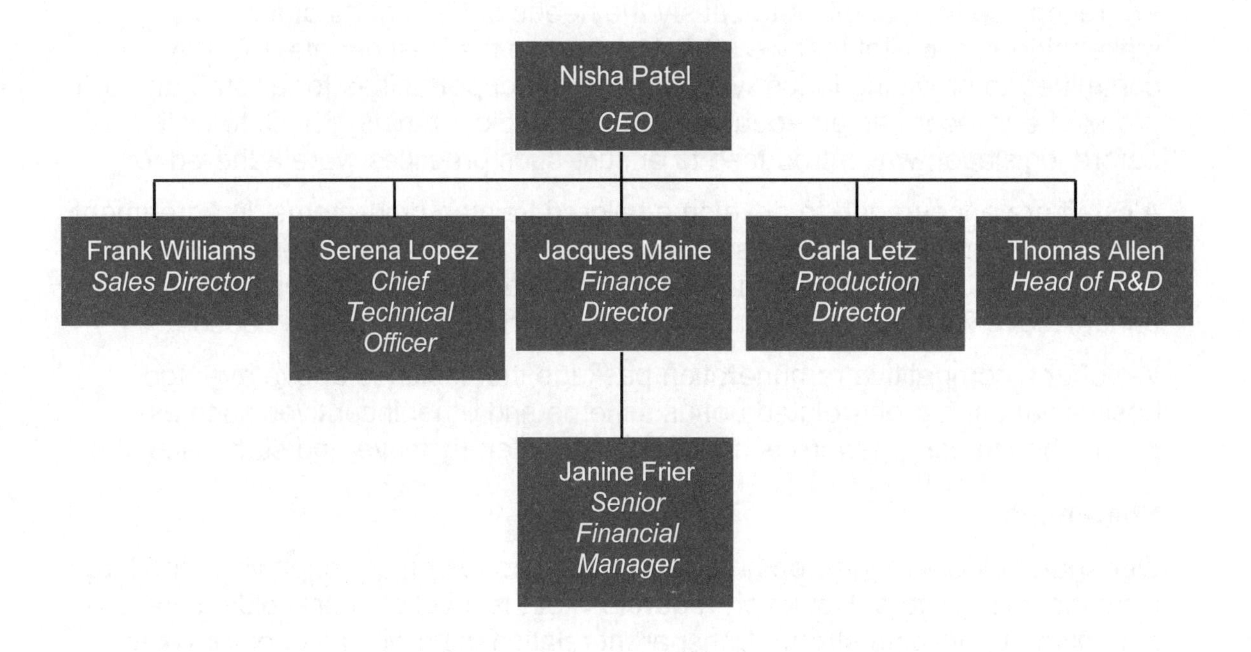

Grainger's sales graph

Grainger is one of the largest global mobile phone manufacturers, expressed in the number of phones sold.

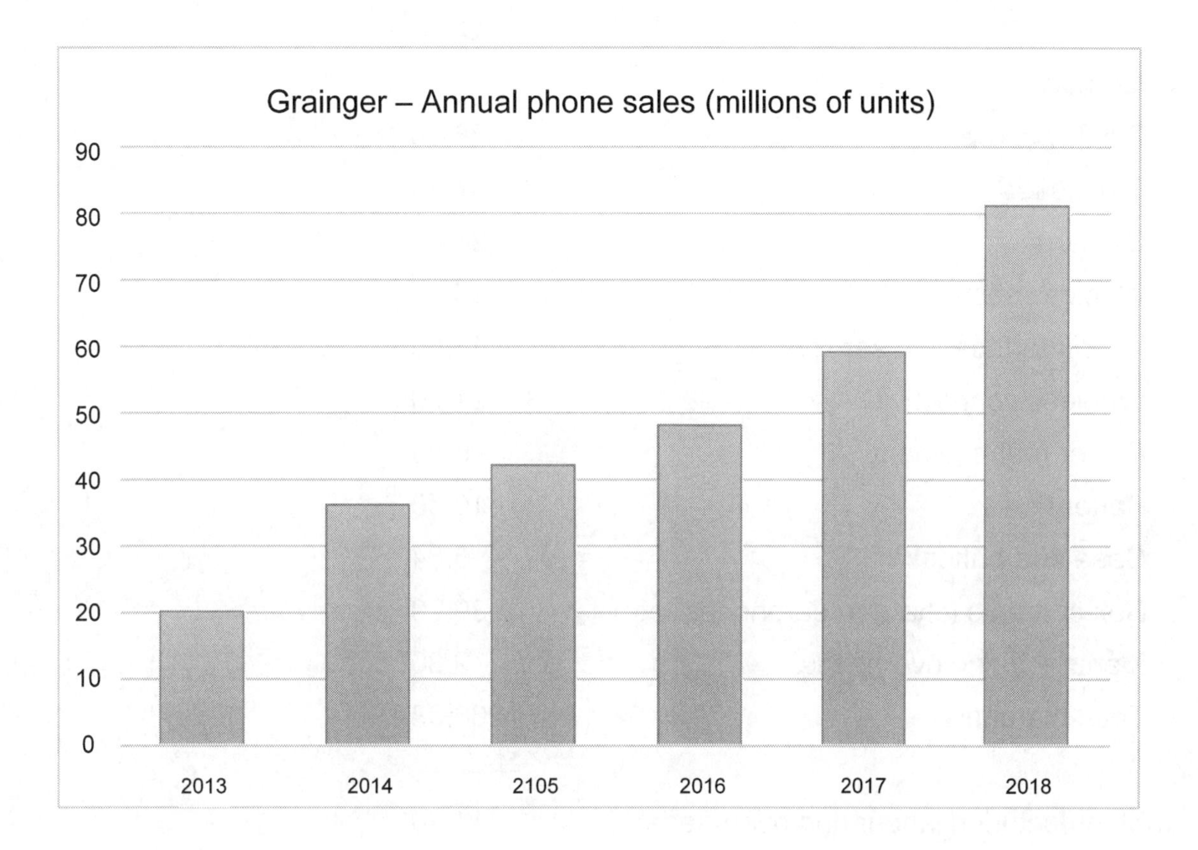

The cost of manufacturing a mobile phone

The cost of manufacturing one of Grainger's most popular models is shown below:

	D$
Memory	
Display screen	28.56
Processor	57.40
Camera	26.60
Wireless section	18.20
User interface and sensors	44.80
Wireless connectivity	21.00
Power management	5.88
Battery	10.50
Case and buttons	5.04
Box contents (charger, earphones, etc)	39.20
Manufacturing overheads	9.80
Total materials	266.98
Manufacturing labour and overheads	11.20
	278.18

Extracts from Grainger's financial statements

Grainger consolidated statement of profit or loss

For the year ended 31 December	2018	2017
	D$ million	D$ million
Revenue	39,712	34,890
Cost of sales	(22,822)	(20,040)
	———	———
Gross profit	16,890	14,850
Research and development expenses	(5,755)	(5,688)
Selling and administrative expenses	(6,053)	(5,948)
	———	———
Operating profit	5,082	3,214
Finance costs	(399)	(262)
	———	———
Profit before tax	4,683	2,952
Tax	(545)	(343)
	———	———
Profit for year	4,138	2,609
	———	———

Grainger consolidated statement of financial position

As at 31 December	2018	2017
	D$ million	D$ million
Non-current assets		
Goodwill and intangible assets	282	266
Property, plant and equipment	3,820	3,422
	4,102	3,688
Current assets		
Inventories	6,233	5,723
Trade receivables	9,249	8,126
Cash and cash equivalents	10,456	7,412
	25,938	21,261
Total assets	30,040	24,949
Equity		
Equity attributable to owners	20,496	17,096
Non-controlling interests	200	187
	20,696	17,283
Non-current liabilities		
Loans	2,614	1,717
Deferred tax	46	38
	2,660	1,755
Current liabilities		
Trade payables	6,133	5,408
Tax	551	503
	6,684	5,911
	30,040	24,949

Note 1 – segmental information

Revenue		
	2018	**2017**
	D$ million	D$ million
Europe	12,708	10,118
Asia	9,531	9,420
America	7,148	6,629
Middle East	4,368	2,791
Other	5,957	5,932
	39,712	34,890
Operating profit		
	2018	**2017**
	D$ million	D$ million
Europe	1,830	996
Asia	1,321	868
America	813	579
Middle East	457	321
Other	661	450
	5,082	3,214

Note 2 – intangibles

	Goodwill	**Development**	**Patents**	**Trademarks**	**Total**
	D$ million	D$ million	D$ million	D$ million	D$ million
Cost					
At 31 December 2017	160	89	78	45	372
Additions	–	30	8	4	42
Disposals	–	–	(11)	(8)	(19)
At 31 December 2018	160	119	75	41	395
Amortisation					
At 31 December 2017	–	55	32	19	106
Charge for year	–	11	7	5	23
Disposals	–	–	(9)	(7)	(16)
At 31 December 2018	–	66	30	17	113
Net book value					
At 31 December 2018	160	53	45	24	282
At 31 December 2017	160	34	46	26	266

Note 3 – property, plant and equipment

	Property	Plant and equipment	Total
	D$ million	D$ million	D$ million
Cost			
At 31 December 2017	1,232	3,901	5,133
Additions	27	722	749
Disposals	–	(267)	(267)
	———	———	———
At 31 December 2018	1,259	4,356	5,615
	———	———	———
Amortisation			
At 31 December 2017	244	1,467	1,711
Charge for year	47	286	333
Disposals	–	(249)	(249)
	———	———	———
At 31 December 2018	291	1,504	1,795
	———	———	———
Net book value			
At 31 December 2018	968	2,852	3,820
	———	———	———
At 31 December 2017	968	2,434	3,422
	———	———	———

Exhibits

Mobile Technology Weekly

Are you DPSA compliant?

The Data Privacy and Security Act (DPSA) was introduced earlier this year by the Deeland Government. This new legislation builds upon the original Data Protection Act that had been in place for over 20 years and attempts to reflect the sheer volume and variety of data being held by organisations, especially relating to their customers, in the ever-evolving digital economy that we find ourselves in today.

The two key areas of focus of the DPSA are to ensure that data held by an organisation is only used for the purposes agreed with the customer (or user) and that the data is protected from unlawful access by third parties.

Although there have been no prosecutions to date under the new legislation, several high profile Deeland-based organisations are currently under investigation for various degrees of data breaches, including mobile network giant Access who, it is alleged, were subject to a major data breach resulting in a third party gaining access to the personal data of over 500,000 customers, including name, address and credit card details, as well as user names and passwords.

A spokesperson for the Deeland Information Office (DIO), who are responsible for overseeing the DPSA, stated that, whilst they couldn't comment on specific ongoing cases, if any organisation was found guilty of an offence of this magnitude, the DIO would consider seeking the highest penalty possible under the act, which is a fine of D$50m or 1% of annual revenue, whichever is greater.

TECHSPOT

HOME BLOG NEWSBUZZ SUPPORT

TOP 3 DEVELOPMENTS IN MOBILE TECH FOR THE COMING YEAR

1 Flexible Phones

New silicon technology is being developed to produce the first mass produced flexi-phones (tablet computers that can be folded and then used as a mobile phone). Currently in production in Asia for first release expected in January 2020, manufactured by AKIZ Tech.

2 Increased durability and waterproofing

New injection moulding technology is being adapted for the mobile phone industry to guarantee total water resistance without comprising lightweight design and phone aesthetics. Currently being developed and tested by Mensica Technology and expected to be in production by late 2019.

3 Convenient Charging Methods

Several phone companies are working on improving how phones are charged, to remove the inconvenience of needing to plug in a phone to charge it. The use of charging ports instead of cables, using built-in wireless charging options, will probably become standard in newer phone models within the next 12 months.

January 2019

Chapter

4

2019 prototype exam – analysis and summary of the pre-seen

Chapter learning objectives

- to understand various techniques and models that can help familiarisation with the pre-seen.

1 The importance of familiarisation

The pre-seen material is released approximately seven weeks before you sit the exam and one of your first tasks will be to analyse the context within which the case is set. Although your responses in the exam will be driven by the unseen material, you will only be able to fully assess the impact of each event on the organisation if you have a sufficient depth of knowledge and awareness of both the organisation and the industry in which it operates.

The purpose of the pre-seen material is to allow you to gain that knowledge and awareness. Remember, you will be acting in the position of a management accountant who works for the organisation in a Financial Manager role. It will therefore be expected that you will have some familiarity with that business and its industry.

It is extremely important that you study the pre-seen material thoroughly before you go into the examination. There are two main reasons for this:

- It will save time in the examination itself if you are already familiar with the pre-seen material (especially in relation to any relevant financial data given).
- It enables you to develop an understanding of the situation facing the organisation in the case study.

You will not be able to respond to the examination tasks from the pre-seen material alone; the additional material given to you in the unseen examination will present significant new information, which may (but not necessarily) alter the situation substantially. Even so, a major step towards success in the examination is a careful study, exploration and understanding of the pre-seen material.

Each set of pre-seen material is different but as a general rule, you can expect the following:

- Industry background
- History of the business
- Key personnel and structure
- Current business/industry issues
- Management accounting information
- Detail on competitors
- Financial Statements
- Press releases

Each of these areas will need reviewing in detail.

You should question what each piece of information tells you, and why the examiner may have given it to you.

2 Exhibit by exhibit analysis

The purpose of this initial stage is to lay a foundation for further analysis. It's more about asking questions than finding solutions. Before you do anything else, you should read the pre-seen material from beginning to end without making any notes, simply to familiarise yourself with the scenario.

Read the material again, as many times as you think necessary, without making notes. You can do this over a period of several days, if you wish.

When you think you are reasonably familiar with the situation described by the material, you should start to make notes. By making notes, you will become more familiar with the detail of the scenario.

- Try to make notes on each paragraph (or each group of short paragraphs) in the pre-seen material.
- Ask yourself "why might the examiner have told me this?" For example, the history of the company is likely to be scene setting. Don't spend too much time questioning and dissecting this type of information. However, information about competitors, management accounting information and the exhibits are likely to be there for a reason.
- Try to make your questions as broad as possible; consider as many different stakeholders as possible and try to put yourself in different positions (say the CEO, a customer, an employee, etc.) to consider the information from different perspectives.

Illustration 1 – Grainger: Introductory overview

Given below is an example of some questions you could ask yourself relating to the Question Tutorial Exam Question Tutorial Exam pre-seen information?

Question	Potential response
What does Grainger do?	Designs and manufactures mobile phones (p3)
What do mobile phone manufacturers concentrate their development on?	Smartphones but there is a market for "basic" models (p6).
What is an "open source operating system"? What is the "downside" of Grainger's operating system being industry standard?	The operating systems owner grants permission to install it free of charge and to adapt it as required. Downside is direct competitors use the same system (p7)

What are the safety concerns for rechargeable batteries?	Produce a fairly high current and heat (p11)

3 Note taking

When you're making notes, try to be as creative as possible. Psychologists tell us that using conventional linear notes on their own use only a small part of our mental capacity. They are hard to remember and prevent us from drawing connections between topics. This is because they seek to classify things under hierarchical headings.

Here are some techniques that candidates find useful. See which ones work for you as you practise on the Question Tutorial Exam case in this text.

Spider diagrams

Spider diagrams (or clustering diagrams) are a quick graphic way of summarising connections between subjects. You cannot put much detail into a spider diagram, just a few key words. However, it does help you to 'visualise' the information in the case material. You must expect to update your spider diagram as you go along and to redraft it when it starts to get too messy. It is all part of the learning process.

Timelines

Timelines are valuable to make sense of the sequence of events in the pre-seen and to understand where the company in the case study presently stands. The case study exam takes place in real time, so you need to be clear how long is likely to elapse between the data in the pre-seen and the actual exam. This is the time period during which the issues facing the company can be incorporated into the unseen material.

Colours

Colours help you remember things you may want to draw upon in the exam room. You could write down all your financial calculations and observations in green whilst having red for organisational and blue for strategic. Some candidates use different colour highlighter pens to emphasise different aspects of the pre-seen material perhaps using the same colour coding suggestion.

Additionally, sometimes making notes in different colours helps you to remember key facts and some of the preparation that you have done using the pre-seen material.

Use whatever colours work for you – but it does help to make notes on both the pre-seen material and the research you do. DO NOT just read the material – you must take notes (in whatever format) and if colours help you to understand and link your research together then use colours.

4 Technical analysis

Now you're reasonably familiar with the material it's time to carry out some technical analysis to help you identify and understand the issues facing the company.

A good starting point is to revise any 'technical' topics that might be relevant. The pre-seen material might make a reference to a particular 'technical' issue such as Balanced Scorecard, TQM, ABC, "Big Data" and so on. Anticipate exam tasks by asking yourself "how" and "why" you would apply these models in the context of the live case.

If you lack confidence on any topic that might be relevant, go back to your previous study materials and revise it if necessary.

Exercise 1 – Grainger: P2 topic analysis

Typical P2 topic areas could include the following.

1 Discuss whether a balanced scorecard approach would be beneficial for Grainger.

2 Discuss the application of target costing and functional analysis for Grainger.

3 Discuss the implications of a lifecycle costing approach for Grainger's marketing strategies.

4 Identify four significant areas of risk for Grainger.

5 Financial analysis

You will almost certainly be given some figures in the pre-seen material. These might relate to the company's profits or losses, or product profitability. There might be statements of profit or loss and statements of financial position for previous years, future business plans, cash flow statements, capital expenditure plans, and so on.

A key part of your initial analysis will be to perform some simple financial analysis, such as financial ratio calculations or a cash flow analysis. These might give you a picture of changes in profitability, liquidity, working capital management or cash flows over time, and will help ensure you have a rounded picture of the organisation's current position.

If a cash flow statement is not provided, it may be worth preparing a summary of cash flows. You may have to make some assumptions if the detailed information isn't provided but even with these, there is great value in appreciating where the money has come from, and where it is being spent.

Financial analysis is important to understanding the position of the organisation. However, candidates must use any pre-seen calculations wisely and not merely throw them into any answer task they are asked which vaguely asks for numbers! Candidates must remember that often they are writing to a more senior finance professional or a board member who will already know the financial [position of the business. Merely re-stating pre-seen calculations without a real justification for doing so is seen as being unprofessional.

Profitability ratios

You might find useful information from an analysis of profit/sales ratios, for:

- the company as a whole
- each division, or
- each product or service.

Profit margins can be measured as a net profit percentage and as a gross profit percentage. You can then look at trends in the ratios over time, or consider whether the margins are good or disappointing.

Analysing the ratio of certain expenses to sales might also be useful, such as the ratio of administration costs to sales, sales and marketing costs to sales or R&D costs to sales. Have there been any noticeable changes in these ratios over time and, if so, is it clear why the changes have happened?

Working capital ratios

Working capital ratios can be calculated to assess the efficiency of working capital management (= management of inventory, trade receivables and trade payables). They can also be useful for assessing liquidity, because excessive investment in working capital ties up cash and slows the receipt of cash.

The main working capital ratios are:

- "inventory days" or the average inventory holding period: a long period might indicate poor inventory management
- "receivable days" or the average time that customers take to pay: a long period could indicate issues with the collection of cash, although would need to consider this in light of the entity's credit terms and industry averages
- "payable days" or the average time to pay suppliers: a long period could indicate cash flow difficulties for the entity, although would need to consider in light of credit terms.

You should be familiar with these ratios and how to calculate the length of the cash cycle or operating cycle.

Cash flow analysis or funding analysis

If the main objective of a company is to maximise the wealth of its shareholders, the most important financial issues will be profitability and returns to shareholders. However, other significant issues in financial strategy are often:

- cash flows and liquidity, and
- funding

A possible cash flow problem occurs whenever the cash flows from operations do not appear to be sufficient to cover all the non-operational cash payments that the company has to make, such as spending on capital expenditure items.

An analysis of future funding can be carried out by looking at the history of changes in the statement of financial position.

Exercise 2 – Grainger: Ratio Analysis

Complete the following table and answer the questions below.

Ratio	*2018*	*2017*
Growth in revenue		
Gross profit margin		
Operating profit margin		
Research and development (%age of revenue)		
Sales and administration (%age of revenue)		
ROCE		
Inventory days		
Receivables days		
Payables days		
Gearing ratio		

Questions

1 Discuss Grainger's financial performance in2018

2 Discuss Grainger's financial position in 2018

3 Comment on Grainger's financial gearing.

6 Industry analysis and research

Why is industry research important?

Remember, part of your preparatory work is to analyse the context within which the case is set. A full analysis is not possible without an understanding of the industry and research may support the information provided in the pre-seen. From this analysis, you may be better able to understand the key issues and address the requirements.

The pre-seen material usually contains a good summary of relevant information about the industry. This can be relied on as accurate at the time it is published and will form the basis of your analysis. At the management level the scope of this industry information will be more detailed than at operational level to reflect the fact that at this level many of the issues arising will have both an external and internal organisational focus. In contrast, at strategic level the industry data provided with the pre-seen will be more detailed and varied to support analysis of the business from a strategic perspective.

You could further research the industry setting for the case you are working on so that you can develop a better understanding of the problems (and opportunities) facing companies in this industry. Hopefully, it will also stop you from making unrealistic comments in your answer on the day of the exam.

Industry research will allow you to add further comments in terms of:

- identifying potential problems currently facing the industry
- identifying the nature of competition and the basis for customer and supplier relationships
- considering the competitive strategies being followed by companies operating in the real world and how they are achieved (e.g. special technologies, use of brands) and whether they could be adopted by the company in the pre-seen
- identifying issues with operational aspects of real world firms.

How to conduct industry research

Remember that at management level you will not be expected to undertake vast amounts of your own research into the industry. Having said that, such research will help you to more fully understand some of the issues affecting the organisation and to put yourself in the shoes of the person that you will need to be in the exam room. Therefore this section will give you some ideas and tools to help with this research.

Your research could incorporate any of the following sources of information:

- *Personal networks / experience*

  If you happen to work in the industry described, then you could talk to colleagues about the case. If not, then perhaps family or friends with relevant experience could help.

  Alternatively, it may be that you have been a customer in the industry described. For the prototype paper, many students would have had experience of being a gym member and so would appreciate some of the issues involved.

- *Using the Internet*

  This is the most convenient and commonly used method of researching the industry, but as noted above, try to target the information you're looking for in order to avoid wasting time. Generally, you will be looking for the following sorts of information:

  – Websites of firms similar to the one(s) in the pre-seen material. This can help you learn about the sorts of products and competitive strategies they follow and may also yield financial information that can be compared with the data in the pre-seen material.

  – Trade journals of the industry in the pre-seen. This will provide information on real world environmental issues facing the business.

  – Articles on the industry in journals and newspapers. These will keep you up to date on developments.

  – Financial statements of real firms, perhaps even calculating key ratios.

Illustration 2 – Grainger: Real world websites

Relevant websites for the mobile phone industry include the following:

Interesting websites:

Major Challenges in the mobile phone industry

http://www.techradar.com/news/mobile-computing/the-most-important-challenges-facing-the-mobile-industry-1252880/2

The "Internet of Things"

https://www.theguardian.com/technology/2015/may/06/what-is-the-internet-of-things-google

Mobile phone safety issues

http://www.nhs.uk/Conditions/Mobile-phone-safety/Pages/QA.aspx

Future developments in mobile phones

http://www.computerweekly.com/feature/Five-tech-trends-that-will-change-the-mobile-world-in-the-next-10-years

Future battery technology

http://www.pocket-lint.com/news/130380-future-batteries-coming-soon-charge-in-seconds-last-months-and-power-over-the-air

7 Ethical analysis

Ethical issues could relate to any of the following areas:

- corporate social responsibility;
- personal ethical behaviour of individuals in the case;
- business ethics.

Before the exam, you should take some time to remind yourself of CIMA's Guidelines on ethical conduct. You can download a copy of the Ethical Guidelines from CIMA's website, if you want to read the full text. Although these are useful, you must remember that the ethical issues in the exam are not necessarily ethical issues facing the management accountant, but more issues facing the business as a whole. An awareness of general 'corporate ethics' and 'corporate and social responsibility' will therefore be beneficial.

Illustration 3 – Grainger: Real world ethical issues

Online research into mobile phones quickly reveals ethical and environmental (and legal) issues. For example,

Ethical issues

http://www.ethicalconsumer.org/ethicalreports/mobilesreport/environment.aspx

8 Position audit

Once you've analysed all of the above you're ready to carry out a position audit.

CIMA defines a position audit as:

Part of the planning process which examines the current state of the entity in respect of:

- resources of tangible and intangible assets and finance,
- products brands and markets,
- operating systems such as production and distribution,
- internal organisation,
- current results,
- returns to shareholders

What you should be attempting to do is stand back so you can appreciate the bigger picture of the organisation. You can do this by considering four main headings – Strengths, Weaknesses, Opportunities and Threats. . Within your SWOT analysis you should look for:

- Threat homing in upon weakness – the potential for failure.
- Threat on a strength – should be able to defend against it but remember competencies slip.
- Opportunity on a strength – areas they should be able to exploit.
- Opportunity on a weakness – areas where they could exploit in the future if they can change.

In addition to preparing a SWOT analysis, it is useful to prepare a two-three page summary of your analysis. Try not to simply repeat information from the pre-seen but add value by including your thoughts on the analysis you've performed.

Exercise 3 – Grainger: SWOT analysis
Perform a SWOT analysis for Grainger.

9 Main issues and précis

Once you've prepared your summary you are finally able to consider the key issues facing the organisation. Your conclusion on the main issues arising from the pre-seen will direct your focus and aid your understanding of potential issues in the exam.

Once you've got a list of the main issues, give yourself more time to think. Spend some time thinking about the case study, as much as you can. You don't have to be sitting at a desk or table to do this. You can think about the case study when you travel to work or in any spare time that you have for thinking.

- When new ideas come to you, jot them down.
- If you think of a new approach to financial analysis, carry out any calculations you think might be useful.

Remember, all of the above preparatory work enables you to feel as if you really are a management accountant working for this organisation. Without the prep, you're unlikely to be convincing in this role.

Illustration 4 – Grainger: Summary

The pre-seen information concerns a company called Grainger that designs and manufactures mobile phones in the country of Deeland.

Subsequent changes in consumer tastes and trends resulted in the product range changing to be focussed completely on mobile phone manufacturer by 1998 under the trading name of Grainger. Grainger is now a global manufacturer of mobile phones and was quoted on the Deeland stock exchange in 1999.

Grainger does not offer mobile phone services but relies entirely on the network providers to make it possible for the mobiles to make and receive calls. This is largely down to the infrastructure which the network providers have created. The complexity and expense associated with establishing such networks creates a very significant barrier to entry into the mobile phone network industry. The network providers offer the mobile phones at significant discounts to their customers and exercise their considerable buying power, (brought about mainly as a consequence of the dependence on their networks for mobile phone functionality), to obtain discounts from the mobile phone manufacturers to enable this to happen.

Each mobile is unique and identified by SIM card which carries the unique identifying data, This allows the manufacturers to "lock" their phones (via an encrypted setting) making them only available for use to customers of the designated network provider and by the same token protect the network provider from customer abuse after the initial purchase discount has been allocated.

It is possible to buy unlocked phones but these are very expensive given that there is no discount applied by the network provider – an Apple iPhone 10 for example will cost £800 SIM free. Mobile phones are sold through a variety of sales channels either via the network providers own or through a range of independent retailers.

In recent years, driven by the flexibility of the underlying technology, mobile phones have gained a wide variety of additional functions including text messaging, internet access for social media and ecommerce, cameras and in addition they have become a fashion item. Clearly this had added to the complexity of functionality and design resulting in the development of "smartphones" on which the manufacturers seem to concentrate their efforts and which requires continual incremental update and redesign. It is important to remember however that a separate market does exist for lees complicated and inexpensive phones.

Mobile phones rely on a further two key aspects to ensure their reliability and functionality, these are the open source operating system and of course batteries. Grainger's use of the former has become the industry standard which has prevented high costs of developing and updating the system but also prevented significant product differentiation given that Grainger's phones and those of their competitors largely look the same.

Further developments in technology are expected with the next generation (5G) of mobile phones expected to be operational by 2020. Although still in the conceptual phase of development, the key goals of 5G faster data speeds; ultra-low latency reducing communication between devices to 0.001 of a second and the drive toward a more connected world, will need the Grainger management team to think carefully regarding future changes and developments and to plan carefully for their successful achievement.

Competition is growing and comes from both new and existing sources. Given that this growth in competition will contribute toward forcing the price of phones down, the control of costs is becoming critical to maintain profitability and establishing the price to be charged for services provided. In addition, the need to understand market trends and maintain innovation in an ever changing and developing market place requires new and up to date products and services to establish and maintain customer loyalty.

Despite revenue gross profit and net profit increasing in the year to 31st December 2018 the figures are now nine months out of date without any management accounts to update the financial picture. The need to take advantage of growing mobile phone technological developments present significant expansion opportunities whilst on the other hand the threats of an increase in competition, high marketing spend amongst rivals, lack of differentiation in products and additional substitutes are prominent. The mitigation of the risks which these threats generate will need careful consideration.

10 Industry research

It is worth noting that research of the industry referred to in the pre-seen is to be encouraged and candidates who read widely will almost certainly benefit.

Some candidates insist on demonstrating that research in the exam, which is only helpful if it is relevant to the task. In other words, if the candidate offers a real-world example to develop an answer then that will almost certainly earn some marks if it is relevant, but it will simply waste time and distract the marker if that example is not relevant to the task

11 Summary

You should now understand what you need to do in order to familiarise yourself with the pre-seen sufficiently.

Test your understanding answers

Exercise 1 – Grainger: P2 topic analysis

1 Discuss whether a balanced scorecard approach would be beneficial for Grainger.

Benefits of using a Balanced Scorecard approach

The Balanced Scorecard reduces over-reliance on financial performance indicators by encouraging the use of non-financial performance indicators alongside the traditional financial measures.

Financial performance indicators alone are considered to have limited use because they:

- Focus on short term/historical performance
- Can be easily manipulated
- Only consider internal factors
- Do not convey the "whole picture"

The Balanced Scorecard approach would encourage the management team to measure performance under four perspectives.

The Financial Perspective is still considered and traditional financial measures are still used, as the primary objective of any business is to maximise shareholders wealth.

However, it also considers performance indicators from the Customer Perspective. This helps Grainger to consider how a key external stakeholder (an 'average' mobile phone user in Deeland, for example) views the business, and ensures that Grainger can focus on customer retention. This will help the business to remain successful in the future.

The Learning and Growth perspective also ensures that Grainger identifies performance measures which can indicate whether they are likely to be successful in the future, by ensuring that they keep up with the competition and industry changes, for example with the impeding move to 5G technology.

Finally, performance indicators from the Internal Business Process Perspective will look at areas such as efficiency and quality which be having an impact on short term results but also identify areas which can be improved in the long term.

2 Discuss the application of target costing and functional analysis for Grainger.

A brief explanation of target costing principles.

When a business introduces a new product into the market place, it can either choose to focus on costs, i.e. work towards the lowest possible manufacturing cost and hopefully be able to set a selling price that achieves a high level of profit, or focus on differentiating its product to make it more attractive to customers.

Target costing concentrates on the cost angle. It aims to reduce the life-cycle costs of the product while ensuring quality, reliability, and other consumer requirements by examining all possible ideas for cost reduction at the product planning, R&D and prototyping phases of production. The target cost is calculated by deducting the target profit from a pre-determined selling price based on customers' views.

Grainger is at the forefront of telephone manufacture, sales, and developing new mobiles. When a new phone is developed, and before production takes place, a target cost exercise can be undertaken to establish what the customer (the end consumer using the phone, in our case) would be willing to pay, and working backwards, Grainger could establish a target cost.

A definition of functional analysis and how it can help in target costing

Functional analysis is used to change production methods and/or reduce expected costs so the target cost is met.

Functional analysis is applied during the development stage of a product and uses the functions of a product as a basis for cost management. Functional Analysis aims to improve profits by attempting to reduce costs and improve profits by adding new features in a cost effective way that are so attractive to customers that profits actually increase. The obvious extra function for a 5G enabled phone is the 'connectivity' function – an increased bandwidth and the ability to be part of an 'Internet of Things' environment.

It would be pointless including "nice to have" features that phone users did not value, did not use, and were not prepared to pay for. When the exercise is completed for the 5G phone, the unnecessary features will removed and an overall target cost will be calculated – it is the cost of the superfluous characteristics that will be removed, but at no expense of functionality.

Brief overview of functional analysis step-by-step approach for Grainger and its 5G enabled mobile.

A complete breakdown is made of the product, for example the forthcoming 5G phone. It means listing all the functions the telephone would perform, and a second, more detailed research investigation is to be undertaken to establish and identify the importance the customer will attach to each feature/function of the telephone.

3 Discuss the implications of a lifecycle costing approach for Grainger's marketing strategies.

Lifecycle and lifecycle costing / impact on marketing strategies

When the latest mobile phone hits the market, Grainger can't merely expect the network providers and other retailers to put it on shelves and hope for sales. Strategic marketing and advertising are needed – and not just upon the phone's launch.

Marketing throughout each phase of a product's lifecycle is imperative to sustaining its relevancy in the market. There are four stages included in a product's lifecycle: introduction, growth, maturity and decline. Sustaining successful marketing throughout all four stages is key to maximise profitability over the whole of the phone's life.

Phase 0: Development

Costs incurred at that development stage include design and quality costs: we ensure that the forthcoming phone will be as easy to manufacture as possible, and be of high quality.

Grainger must develop a product that has quality from the very start, and whose features meet market requirements. Saving on quality conformance costs is not an option: a defective phone can damage the reputation of the whole company.

Phase 1: Introduction

Introducing a product as innovative as our latest 4G/5G handset requires awareness among early adopters. Early adopters are design and /or tech savvy customers who regard their phone as fashion accessories and want to remain abreast of current trends. These customers may be new, or current users of a Grainger's existing phones.

Therefore, in terms of marketing strategy and related costs, we market our latest phone by appealing to existing users. To achieve this, we incur the costs of a commercial /advertising campaigns in our different markets, to spread the word.

The other substantial costs incurred here are supply chain costs, especially as we are a global player. At introduction stage, the manufacturing challenge is to increase production from a prototype phone to a large volume in a very short time; we have to incur the costs of providing the retailers with the handsets all over the world. Failure to satisfy the immediate demand means sales lost to other competitors, and lost market share.

Phase 2: Growth

In the last two years, Grainger has sold over 140 million devices. In a growth phase, Grainger's tactics are simple: captivating advertising and an unmatched online/shop-based retail user experience. The growth phase of the product lifecycle is all about increasing market share. Achieving this is no easy feat, as it involves pushing into new markets and uses for the phone, and expanding product lines.

Phase 3: Maturity

This is the phase when competitors start to offer competing products. It is then that Grainger concentrates on small, incremental development efforts such as upgrades and add-on features to existing models with costs incurred because of small improvements, a slightly better camera or a more attractive case. So, the costs incurred here are to do with extending life through design enhancements. This, hopefully, should help with getting new customers in untapped markets, and with protecting our market share.

Phase 4: Decline

This phase is known for innovation (looking into the 2020 horizon and focusing on 5G handsets for us now), redesign and functionality changes. We scale down production of the current phone in an orderly manner, whilst maintaining profitability for as long as possible.

4 Identify four significant areas of risk for Grainger.

- Increased competitive pressure from rival phone manufacturers
- Failure of operating systems – mobile phone usage is entirely dependent on the successful operation of these information systems
- Breach of data security – unauthorised access or loss of information could lead to legal claims, disruption to operations and reputational damage.
- Health and safety – serious injury to a customer through failure of battery technology.

Exercise 2 – Grainger: Ratio Analysis

Complete the following table and answer the questions below.

Ratio	*2018*	*2017*
Growth in revenue	+13.8%	
Gross profit margin	42.5%	42.6%
Operating profit margin	12.8%	9.2%
R&D (%age of revenue)	14.5%	16.3%
Sales and admin (%age of revenue)	15.2%	17.0%
ROCE	21.8%	16.9%
Inventory days	100 days	104 days
Receivables days	85 days	85 days
Payables days	98 days	98 days
Gearing ratio	11.2%	9.0%

Questions

1 Discuss Grainger's financial performance in 2018

The revenue of Grainger has increased significantly by 13.8% in 2018 compared to the previous year, with post tax profit increasing by a substantial 56.8%. This indicates very strong profitability and cost control.

Gross profit margin has remained constant at a very healthy 42.5%. Operating profit margin has increased from 9.2% to 12.8% indicating that the growth in profits has at least been in part due to cost control. Pre-tax margin has shown similar improvement increasing from 8.5% to 11.8%

Both research & development and selling & administrative costs have increased by less than 2% on 2017. In terms of research and development it may be that 2018 is now seeing the benefits in terms of revenue growth from research and development activities that have been expensed in previous years.

The growth in revenue is substantial enough to suggest an increase in sales volumes rather than purely increased prices. In turn, this would lead to economies of scale being gained within administrative expenses and so explain the increase in operating profit margin.

The increase in profit margins has been the driving force behind the increased return on capital employed from 16.9% to 21.8%.

2 Discuss Grainger's Financial Position in 2018.

Financial position

Current and quick ratios have both increased in 2018 and seem to be at very healthy levels. Indeed it may be argued that they are too high and that cash resources in particular could be better utilised. Cash & cash equivalent balances have increased by 41% – D$7,412m to D$10,456m indicating the strong liquidity position of Grainger.

Inventory days are constant at approximately 100 days. On the one hand many of the raw material components of mobile phones may not suffer high obsolescence risk in terms of being perishable, components may suffer technical obsolescence risk. Grainger will need to ensure that they are not exposed to potential write offs due to holding technically obsolete components, in particular batteries, display screens and cameras.

Receivables days initially appear high at 85 days. However, this may be the norm for the industry as retailers are likely to only pay Grainger once they have sold the handsets in their stores. Additionally Grainger do not have cashflow pressures that create the need to chase retailers for prompt payment.

Payables days are also high at 98 days. Grainger are perhaps able to use their power as one of the largest mobile phone manufacturers to extend their credit facilities with suppliers. It is also likely to be as a consequence of collecting cash quite slowly from customers that suppliers are then also paid slowly. However, given their high cash reserves there is no reason for Grainger to pay suppliers so slowly if they do not wish to do so.

It should be noted that whilst payables days has been calculated, the ratio may be distorted. As a manufacturing business, Grainger's cost of sales figure is likely to include many production costs such as wages, depreciation and other manufacturing overheads as well as the simple purchase of raw materials. Thus caution should be exercised in the use of the payables days' calculation.

3 Comment on Grainger's financial gearing

Gearing

The gearing ratio of Grainger has increased from 9% to 11.2%. There has been an increase in loans of nearly D$900m, which has significantly increased debt levels by just over 50% when compared to 2017.

It is likely that this debt was used to finance the investment in property, plant and equipment of D$749 m and expenditure of D$42m on intangible assets (mainly development expenditure).

Overall the absolute levels of debt seem very moderate and gearing seems quite low, especially for a manufacturing business. The high retention of profits has increased equity such that there has been a relatively small increase in gearing.

The high cash balances of the entity suggest that significant levels of debt finance are not required.

Conclusion

Overall there has been significant growth in the profitability of Grainger and both the short-term and long-term position of the group seems strong.

Exercise 3 – Grainger: SWOT analysis

SWOT Analysis

STRENGTHS

- Established business – 60+ years
- Profitable business
- Strong cash position
- Large customer base
- Strong sales growth
- Listed – ability to raise finance
- Strong brand
- Experienced management team
- RND Department
- Global distribution network
- Industry standard operating system

WEAKNESSES

- Dependency on network providers
- No obvious change management department
- No obvious risk management function
- Potential capacity issues
- Potential communication issues with global coverage
- High loan finance – (low but increasing gearing)
- Cash management?
- Potential supply chain issues
- Governance issues i.e. no NED's shown
- No specific IT function
- Potential issues with customer knowledge
- Pricing strategy – low profitability in Middle East
- Focus on too many products

OPPORTUNITIES

- Product Development
- "Application" development e.g. better cameras; waterproof phones
- Expansion options in Deeland – joint ventures
- Global expansion of Grainger brand – geographic expansion/acquisition
- Growing market for 5G "the internet of things"
- Improvements in performance measurement
- Improvements in risk management
- Incremental product updates

THREATS

- Rapid technological change
- Market is becoming saturated in developed countries
- Lack of product differentiation
- Loss of key staff to competitors
- Increasing competition
- Supply issues for key components
- Foreign exchange risk
- Growth of lower cost substitutes – e.g. Wi-Fi phones, Skype
- Cultural threat via geographical expansion plans
- Slow recovery of world economy
- Phone security/fraud
- Potential legal claims – breach of compliance
- Battery safety
- Poor customer service/support, damaging reputation

Chapter

5

Exam day techniques

Chapter learning objectives

- To develop a carefully planned and thought through strategy to cope with the three hours of exam time

1 Exam day strategy

Once you have studied the pre-seen, learnt the three subject syllabi thoroughly and practised lots of exercises and mocks, you should be well prepared for the exam.

However, it is still important to have a carefully planned and thought through strategy to cope with those three hours of exam time.

This chapter takes you through some of the key skills to master to ensure all your careful preparation does not go to waste.

2 Importance of time management

Someone once referred to case study exams as "the race against time" and it's difficult to imagine a more accurate description. Being able to do what the examiner is wanting is only half of the battle; being able to deliver it in the time available is another matter altogether. This is even more important than in previous exams you may have faced because each section in the real exam is now timed and that once that time is up you will be moved on. Case study is not like a traditional exam where you can go back to a question if you get extra inspiration or feel you have some time left over. You have to complete each task within the time stated.

For this reason, time management is a key skill required to pass the Case Study Examination.

Successful time management requires two things:

- A tailored time plan – one that plays to your personal strengths and weaknesses; and
- Discipline in order to stick to it!

Time robbers

There are a number of ways in which time can be wasted or not used effectively in the Case Study Examination. An awareness of these will help to ensure you don't waste time in your exam.

Inactive reading

The first part of each task must be spent actively reading, processing the information and considering the impact on the organisation, how the issues link together and what could be done to resolve them. You may not have time to have a second detailed read and so these thoughts must be captured first time around.

Too much time spent on presentation

You will be writing your answer in software with some similarities to Microsoft Word however the only functions available are

- Cut
- Copy
- Paste
- Undo
- Redo
- Bold
- Italic
- Underline

The temptation to make various words bold or italics or underlined, is very hard to resist. But, resist you must! There are very few marks available for having a response that is well presented, and these finer details will be worth nothing at all.

Being a perfectionist

Students can often spend such a long time pondering about what to write that over the course of a 3 hour exam, over half of it is spent staring into space.

As you are sitting a computer exam you not only spend time pondering, but also have the ability to delete so can change your mind several times before settling on the right word combinations. Just focus on getting your points down and don't worry about whether they could have been phrased better.

Although do bear in mind that the marker has to be able to read and understand your answer, so do write in clear English.

Too much detail on earlier parts of the requirement

As we've said earlier, not finishing answers is a key reason for failing the Case Study Examination. One of the main reasons why students fail to finish a section is a lack of discipline when writing about an issue. They feel they have to get all of their points down rather than selecting the better points and moving on. If a task requires you to discuss three different areas it is vital that you cover all parts adequately.

A key skill is selecting and writing about the key points and NOT taking a scattergun approach to an answer.

A key determinant of a professional answer is those that are clearly focused on the most relevant points.

Too much correction

Often students can re-read paragraphs three or more times before they move on to writing the next part of their answer. Instead, try to leave the read through until the final few minutes of the task and try to correct as many obvious errors as possible. The CIMA marker will be reading and marking your script on screen and it is harder to read and understand the points you are making if there are many typing errors.

3 Assimilation of information

One of the most challenging things to deal with in a case study examination is the volume of information which you have available. This is particularly difficult when you have both pre-seen and unseen information to manage and draw from. It is important that you refer to relevant pre-seen information in your responses as well as incorporating the unseen information.

The key things that you need to do to assimilate the information effectively and efficiently are:

- Read about and identify each event
- Consider what the issue is
- Evaluate the impact of the issue. Who is affected, by how much are they affected and what would happen if no action was taken?
- Determine the most useful and relevant exhibits from the pre-seen

Capturing all of your thoughts and ideas at this stage can be difficult and time consuming.

The following section on planning your answer will show you how to do this effectively without wasting time or effort.

4 Planning your answers

In section 2 of this chapter we saw how important it was to manage your time in the exam to ensure you're able to complete all of the necessary stages in the preparation of your answer.

One important aspect of your exam is planning your answer. Sitting the case study exam is not as straight forward as turning up, reading the requirements, and then writing your answer.

If you do attempt to write without any form of content plan, your response will lack direction and a logical flow, it won't fully address the key points required and any recommendations will lack solid justification. It is for this reason that time should be specifically allocated to planning the content of your answers.

Given the preparation you've done before the exam, reading the unseen can often feel like a firework display is happening in your brain; each new piece of information you read about triggers a series of thoughts and ideas.

The planning process must therefore begin as soon as you start reading the unseen information. Every second counts within the case study exam and so it's important to use all of your time effectively by capturing the thoughts as they come to you.

To make sure the time spent now is of use to you throughout the task, you will need consider carefully how best to document your thoughts. You will be provided with an on-screen notes page ('scratchpad') as well as a wipe-clean laminated notes page and marker pen. Any method you adopt to plan must be concise whilst still allowing you to capture all of your ideas and see the bigger picture in terms of how the issues interrelate with one another (see additional guidance below). Furthermore, the method must suit you! Everyone is different and what might work for one person could be a disaster for another. For example, some people prefer to work with lists, others with mind maps.

Most people find that some form of central planning sheet (to enable the bigger picture to be seen) is best. How you prepare the central planning sheet is a matter of personal preference and we've given illustrations of two different methods below. Practise each one to find out which you prefer and then tailor it further to settle on something that works for you.

Method 1 – The ordered list

This process is ideally suited to people who prefer lists and structure.

Step 1:

- Begin by reading everything in the task exhibit
- Ensure you have identified all aspects of the task and then write this on the left hand side of your planning sheet

Step 2:

- Read everything in the trigger exhibit, making notes next to the relevant task

Step 3:

- Review your list to identify any linkages to information provided in the pre-seen and note next to the task on your planning sheet

Step 4:

- Brainstorm any technical knowledge you can use in responding to the task and note this on your planning sheet

Illustration 1 – Planning

On Monday morning your boss arrived in work full of enthusiasm for a new business venture he had thought of over the weekend. This was in response to a conversation that had taken place at Friday night drinks when the CEO expressed concern that she felt the business was stagnating and needed some new products to rekindle customer interest.

Your boss needed to harness his ideas and put together an outline plan for a mid-morning coffee meeting with the CEO. Typically, the idea had germinated without sufficient thought and you were asked to consider the critical factors that needed to be considered in launching the new product and write a briefing document for the meeting.

Requirement:

Prepare a plan for your briefing document.

Solution

Critical factors	*Goals and objectives*	*Skills and experience*	*Finance*	*Marketing and sales*
New product	Matches mission and objectives?	Experience in manufacturing?	Available finance?	Advertising
	Strengths?	Available labour?	Investment?	Social media
			Working capital?	Website?
Technical content?				4Ps

Method 2 – The extended mind map

This process is ideally suited to those who prefer pictures and diagrams to trigger their thoughts.

Step 1:

- Read the unseen information and identify the key tasks required
- As you read, write each task in a "bubble" on your planning sheet.

Step 2:

- Keep adding each new part of the task you identify to your sheet. At the end you should have a page with a number of bubbles dotted about.

Step 3:

- Review your bubbles to identify any linkages to the trigger information or pre-seen exhibits. Add any relevant information to your planning sheet in a bubble attached to the appropriate part of the task.

Step 4:

- Review the task bubbles and brainstorm any relevant knowledge which you can use in responding to the task. Add this to bubbles attached to the task.

With detailed information provided in the exam it would be very likely that your brain would think of a wide range of ideas which, if left uncaptured, would be forgotten as quickly as you thought of them.

This is where mind mapping comes in handy. You would not of course need to draw one as neat as this and feel free to add colours or graphics to help your thought processes.

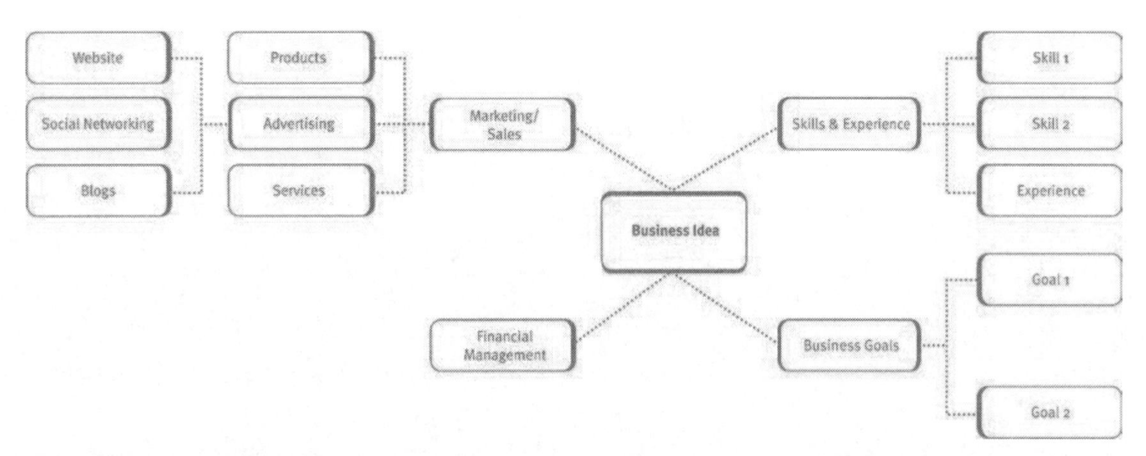

Why not try putting your thoughts on the previous illustration into a mind map like the one above?

NB: Using the software for planning and structure

Some candidates might find the methods suggested above to be too complex and time consuming. For example, a 45 minute task with at least two requirements allows a maximum of 27 minutes (60% of 45) available for any given requirement and possibly much less.

While planning is thoroughly recommended because it is a very good technique and will provide candidates with a framework for future career challenges, to save time it is possible to type subheadings while thinking, use cut and paste to get them in the right order and then use that structure to type up the answer.

This approach is developed more in the section on "Examiner Comments" in Chapter 7.

Some additional guidance

(1) This is perhaps the hardest part of the exam; as soon as you tell your brain it needs to come up with some ideas, it very often refuses to cooperate! Practice makes perfect so working through the exercises in Chapter 7 and attempting mock exams will really help your brain to deliver ideas when you need it to.

(2) Don't simply view technical models as something that must be included to tick a box if explicitly requested in the requirements. Instead use the models to help analyse the issues, suggest solutions or generate ideas. They were developed to be useful! Don’t describe models – apply them!

(3) If you start looking at one of the task requirements and are stuck for ideas, don't waste time staring into space. Move on to the next part of the task (but not onto the next task itself as you won’t be able to return) and you'll find the creative juices soon start flowing.

Have a go!

5 Communication skills

The case study examinations aim to test a wide range of skills and you may be required to communicate in many different ways to various different audiences, each with different information needs.

In Management Case Study, the best advice is to write your response clearly, in short sentences and making use of paragraphs to offer a logical flow. This will apply to whatever format is required for your response.

6 Writing style

Introduction

Writing style is something that develops over time. It is influenced by your education and experiences. To some it comes easily, they enjoy words – but remember, you are not looking to win any prizes in literature. It's about putting facts, ideas and opinions in a clear, concise, logical fashion. Some students get very worried about their writing styles. As a general rule you should try to write as you would talk. But a formal report to a senior colleague (such as a director) would certainly not be written like this. It must be formal and in an appropriate tome. Being professional is critical.

Logical flow

A typical point starts with a statement of fact, either given in the case or derived from analysis – 'what?'

This can then be followed by an interpretation – 'so what?'

This can then lead to an implication – 'now what?', or 'what next?'

For example:

(1) What? – The net relevant cash flow for the project is positive.

(2) So what? – Suggesting we should go ahead with the project.

(3) Now what? – Arrange board meeting to discuss strategic implications.

A similar structure can be obtained using the Socratic approach – what, why, how?

- So what?
- Why should we use it?
- How does it work?

Who is reading the response?

Failure to pitch the level correctly will inevitably result in failure to communicate your ideas effectively, since the reader will either be swamped with complexity, or bored with blandness. The recipients of the report should also dictate the wording and language used in the candidate's response, being careful not to allocate blame (unless you have been asked to do so).

For example:

Tactless	*Tactful*
The directors have clearly made errors	There were other options open to the board that, with hindsight, would have been beneficial
The marketing director is responsible for this disastrous change in strategy	The board should consider where this went wrong? It would appear that the marketing department may have made some mistakes

Making your response easy to read

To ensure that the marker finds your answers accessible and easy to read, you should try to do the following:

- Use short words, short sentences, short phrases and short paragraphs. If you are adopting the 'what, so what, what now' approach, then you could have a paragraph containing three sentences. The next point can then be a new paragraph, also containing three sentences.
- Use the correct words to explain what you mean! For example, students often get confused between:
  - recommendations (what they should do – actions) and options (what they could do – possibilities).
  - objectives (what we want to achieve – the destination) and strategies (how we intend to achieve them – the route).
- Avoid using vague generalisations. Too often students will comment that an issue will "impact" on profit rather than being specific about whether profit will increase or decrease (or even better still, trying to quantify by how much). Other common phrases which are too vague include "communicate with" (you need to say specifically what should be discussed) and "look in to" (how should an option be looked in to?)
- Avoid unnecessary repetition. This can either be of information from the exam paper (pre-seen or unseen), of discussion within the report (in particular between what is said in one section and another) or can relate to the words that you use. Some students fall into the trap of thinking that writing a professional report means simply writing more words to say the same thing! The issue is quality not quantity.

  For example, compare the following:

  - 'I, myself, personally' OR 'I'

- 'export overseas' OR 'export'
- 'green in colour' OR 'green'

- Watch your spelling – this may seem a small and unimportant point, but poor spelling makes a document seem sloppy and may convey an impression that the content is as loose as the general appearance! Poor spelling interrupts the marker as they read your report, so there is the danger that they conclude that it did not have a logical flow.
- Recommendations – be decisive – do not 'sit on the fence' or ask for more information. Make a clear recommendation based on the information you have and justify why you have chosen that course of action.

Exercise 1

This exercise will get you thinking about what makes a well written script. The technical content of the requirement is not relevant – we are focusing on writing style and flow.

The risk committee of X plc met to discuss a report by its risk manager. The report focused on a number of risks that applied to a chemicals factory recently acquired in another country.

She explained that the new risks related to the security of the new factory in respect of burglary, the supply of one of the key raw materials that experienced fluctuations in world supply and also an environmental risk.

The environmental risk was with respect to the possibility of poisonous emissions from the new factory. The CEO who chaired the risk committee, said that the factory was important to him for two reasons. First, he said it was strategically important to the company. Second, it was important because his own bonuses depended upon it. He said that he knew from the report what the risks were, but that he wanted somebody to explain to him what strategies they could use to manage the risks. 'I don't get any bonus at all until we reach a high level of output from the factory,' he said. 'So I don't care what the risks are, we will have to manage them.'

You have been asked to outline strategies that can be used to manage risk and identify, with reasons, an appropriate strategy for each of the three risks facing the new venture.

Requirement:

Consider these two responses and note the positive and negative aspects of each.

Answer 1

Introduction

Risk can be managed using the following strategies.

- **Transfer** the risk to another organisation for example by buying insurance. This is usually cost effective where the probability of the risk is low but the impact is potentially high.
- **Avoid** the risk altogether by withdrawing completely from the risky activity. This is done where the risk is high probability and high frequency and so it is too costly to reduce the risk sufficiently.
- **Reduce** the risk by implementing controls or by diversification.
- **Accept** the risk without taking any further steps to mitigate it. For this to be acceptable the frequency and the impact of the risk must place the risk within the risk appetite of the company.

Risk of burglary

It is usual to insure against burglary an example of the transfer strategy. This is because of the high impact of burglary.

It is also usual to put safeguards in place such as security guards because of the probability of burglary. This is an example of risk reduction.

Raw materials supply fluctuation

Depending on the cost benefit analysis the company could chose to transfer the risk by entering into forward contracts to purchase the materials.

There will be a cost associated with this and it will lower but not remove the risk associated with supply and price fluctuations. They may choose to accept the risk as part of the operational risk associated with their industry.

Environmental risk

The company should take reasonable steps to reduce the chance poisonous emissions. It should use appropriate technology and controls to reduce the risk.

Risks cannot be completely eliminated so if the poisonous emissions could give rise to significant costs it should also purchase insurance and transfer the risk.

Answer 2

Risk is managed by this:

(1) Identify the risk. This is by brainstorming all the things that the risk can be.

(2) Risk assessment. We won't know this properly until afterwards.

(3) Risk Profiling. This is decided on consequences and impact.

(4) Risk quantification. This can be average loss or it can be largest loss.

(5) Risk consolidation which will depend on the risk appetite and diversification.

The risks at the factory are:

- The main risk at the factory is environmental risk. You can't do anything about this risk because global warming is because of everyone.
- The big risk is that the CEO is "I don't care what the risks are" this will need to have the risk awareness embedded in and the tone at the top.
- The other risk is that the CEO could manipulate the output levels to get his bonus. This needs to be looked at seriously because he is also on the risk committee and the remuneration committee and he is not independent and that should be a NED.

7 Summary

You should have an appreciation of some of the issues you may encounter in the exam and some possible techniques to overcome these.

Next steps:

(1) In the next two chapters we will present the unseen and guide you through the process of producing an answer. It is worth ensuring you can log on to the Pearson Vue site now and make sure you have registered for the practice case study exam. It is advisable to familiarise yourself with the software as much as possible.

(2) As you are about to embark on a full attempt at the paper it is a good time to revisit previous chapters and ensure you are comfortable with all of the material so far before proceeding.

Test your understanding answers

Exercise 1

The first solution has several positive aspects:

- Brief introduction linking to requirement
- Overview of model with explanation and clear examples
- Specific points from scenario addressed
- Headings clearly signpost the answer
- Appropriate language

There are some areas which could be improved:

- Specific reference to the company name
- More explicit use of the information from the scenario

The second solution is not as strong as the first. Some of the main criticisms:

- Main options available are not clearly explained
- No attempt to introduce the answer
- Inappropriate language for a formal report/response
- Lack of tact regarding the CEO – the intended audience!!

As a piece of writing there is not much to say from a positive perspective except:

- Clear structure
- Writing is concise (but probably a bit too brief)

Chapter

6

Prototype exam variant 1 – walkthrough

Chapter learning objectives

- To gain experience trying to answer a case study exam.

1 The aim of a walkthrough

The aim of this chapter is to give you a chance to practise many of the techniques you have been shown in previous chapters of this study text. This should help you to understand the various thought processes needed to complete the full three hour examination. It is important that you work through this chapter at a steady pace.

Don't rush on to the next stage until you have properly digested the information, followed the guidance labelled 'Stop and Think!' and made your own notes. This will give you more confidence than simply reading the model solutions. You should refer to the unseen produced in the previous chapter as you proceed through these exercises.

The following chapter will then guide you through the suggested solutions and marking key.

2 First screen

The opening screen of the exam shows you how many sub-tasks you have to deal with and how to allocate your time within tasks:

Section (task)	Time for section (minutes)	Number of answer screens	Number of sub-tasks	% time to spend on each sub-task
1	45	1	2	(a) 50% (b) 50%
2	45	1	2	(a) 60% (b) 40%
3	45	1	2	(a) 40% (b) 60%
4	45	1	2	(a) 50% (b) 50%

The exam software will prevent you from spending more than 45 minutes on task 2, say, but you need to ensure that this is split 27 minutes on sub-task (a) and 18 minutes on sub-task (b)

3 Task 1

Understanding the context

The first two screens of task 1 reveal that Grainger has decided to launch a new model of smartphone.

For task 1, the trigger and requirements are mixed together into one screen, together with reference material:

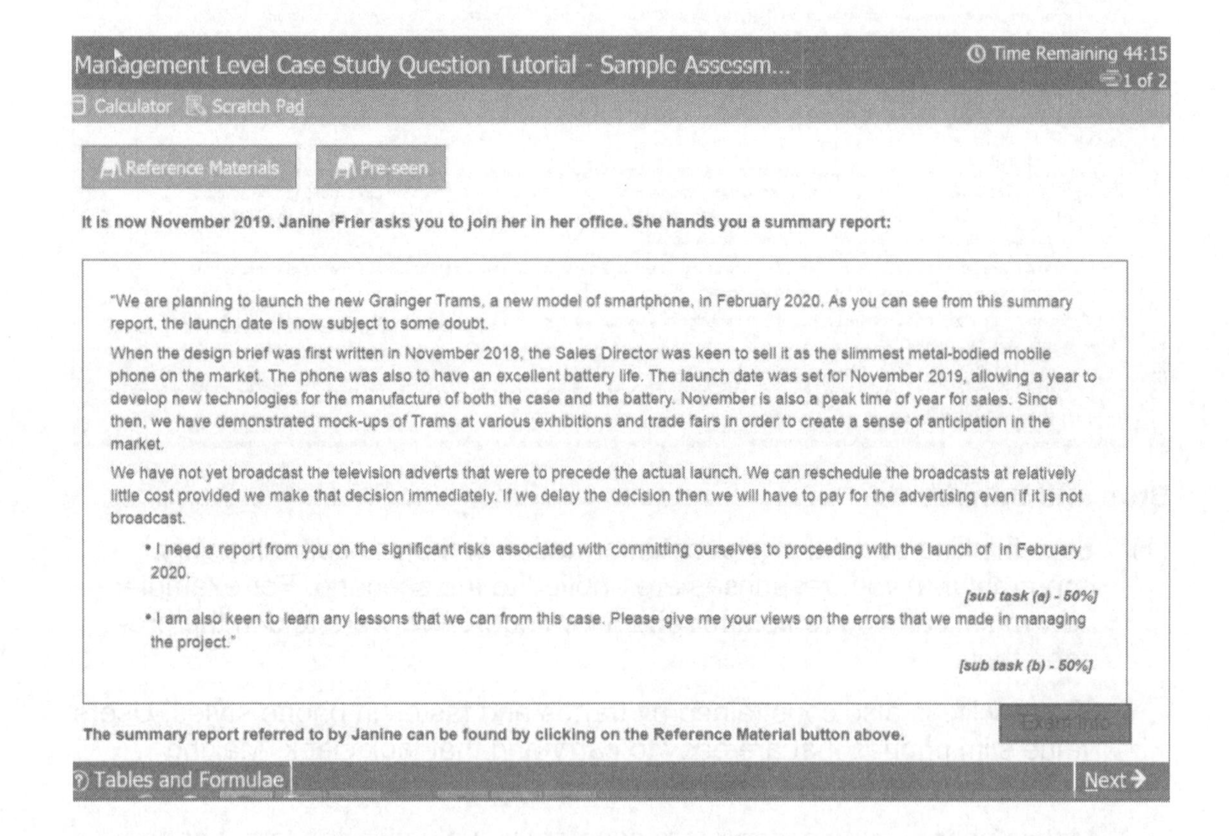

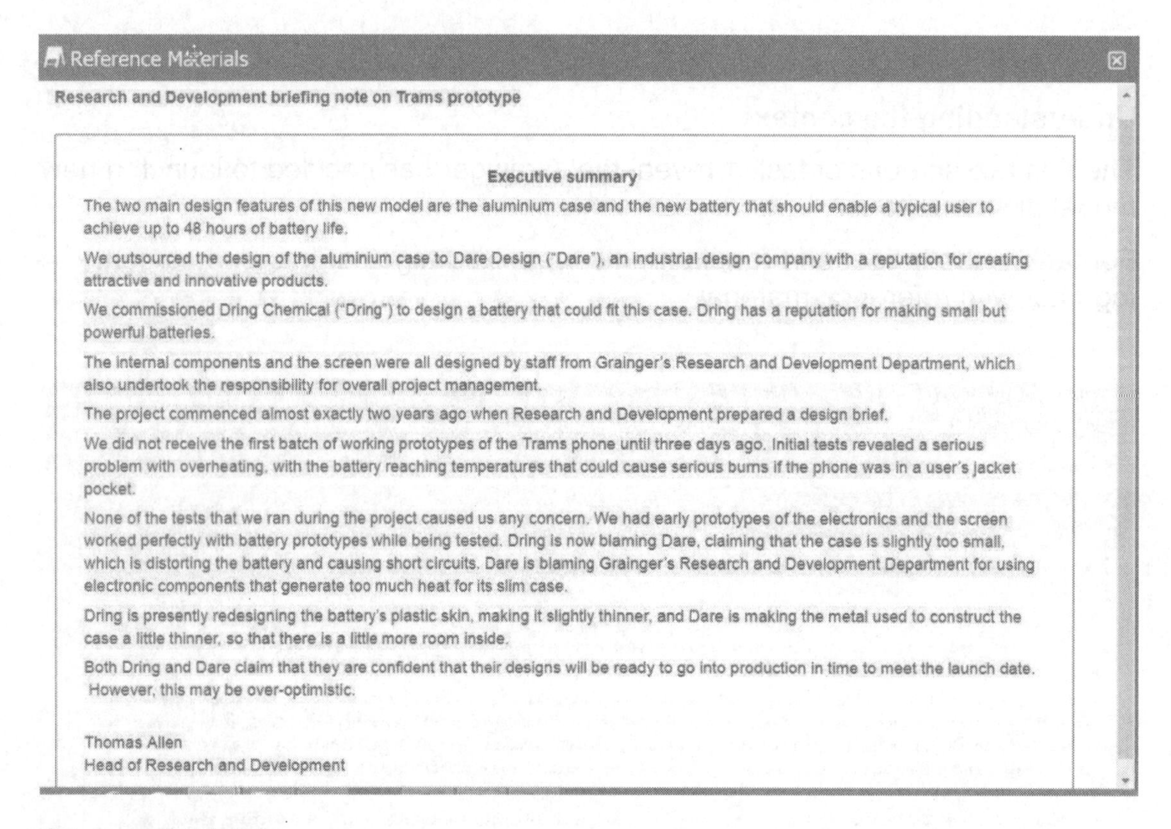
Reference Materials

Research and Development briefing note on Trams prototype

Executive summary

The two main design features of this new model are the aluminium case and the new battery that should enable a typical user to achieve up to 48 hours of battery life.

We outsourced the design of the aluminium case to Dare Design ("Dare"), an industrial design company with a reputation for creating attractive and innovative products.

We commissioned Dring Chemical ("Dring") to design a battery that could fit this case. Dring has a reputation for making small but powerful batteries.

The internal components and the screen were all designed by staff from Grainger's Research and Development Department, which also undertook the responsibility for overall project management.

The project commenced almost exactly two years ago when Research and Development prepared a design brief.

We did not receive the first batch of working prototypes of the Trams phone until three days ago. Initial tests revealed a serious problem with overheating, with the battery reaching temperatures that could cause serious burns if the phone was in a user's jacket pocket.

None of the tests that we ran during the project caused us any concern. We had early prototypes of the electronics and the screen worked perfectly with battery prototypes while being tested. Dring is now blaming Dare, claiming that the case is slightly too small, which is distorting the battery and causing short circuits. Dare is blaming Grainger's Research and Development Department for using electronic components that generate too much heat for its slim case.

Dring is presently redesigning the battery's plastic skin, making it slightly thinner, and Dare is making the metal used to construct the case a little thinner, so that there is a little more room inside.

Both Dring and Dare claim that they are confident that their designs will be ready to go into production in time to meet the launch date. However, this may be over-optimistic.

Thomas Allen
Head of Research and Development

Stop and think!

(1) Start thinking about the relevant information in the pre-seen. It's very important that your responses are applied to the scenario. For example, how much can you remember about Grainger? We were told in the pre-seen that:

"Battery life is also constrained by trends and tastes in phone styles. Users value slim phones that are easy to carry and that look sleek. Making phones slimmer leaves less internal volume for a large battery.

Mobile phone manufacturers are constantly evaluating the latest battery technology because users are often frustrated by their phones running out of charge. It is not uncommon for users to be forced to recharge their phones every night in order to obtain a full day's use next day.

Rechargeable batteries can create problems for manufacturers and users. They produce a fairly high current and the process of charging and discharging rechargeable batteries can also create a great deal of heat. That can raise safety concerns. For example, fuel stations forbid the use of mobile phones while operating fuel pumps because of the slight risk of a spark created by a rechargeable battery igniting the vapour from the car's fuel tank".

(2) Grainger is set to launch a new phone with a case which is slightly too small, distorting the battery and causing short circuits. This in turn is creating a significant risk with a product that already has questionable functionality and bad press.

(3) There could be integration issues when combing the significance of project management (E2) and risk (E2; P2)

Answering the question set – understanding the requirements

The requirements (and further context) are given on the first screen with reference material indicating the process that took place during the development of the prototype:

It is vital that you understand the nature and scope of the requirements. Here you need to prepare a report which covers:

- "I need a report from you on the significant risks associated with committing ourselves to proceeding with the launch in February 2020"

  Make sure you answer the question set – we need to be sure that we cover the risks which specifically relate to the immediate launch rather than a discussion covering generic risks. Similarly it would be good practice to consider both "upside" and "downside" risk

- "I am also keen to learn any lessons that we can from this case. Please give me your views on the errors that we made in managing the project."

  You need to make clear the failing within the management of the project, the effect of these failings and lesson that can be learned for future projects. Application of good project management to the scenario is vital rather than stating the steps usually associated with best practice.

Let's plan – Task 1(a)

If you prefer to plan within your answer box, then the above considerations will help you set up suitable headings and then start to populate them.

Alternatively, if you prefer to use your wipe clean whiteboard, then you could split your planning sheet into a grid to ensure all parts are covered, for example:

Type of risk	*Effect*
Safety of the phone – launch before issues are resolved	– Personal injury – Liability – Reputation
Phone failure – issue with modifications	– Unreliable products – Reputation – Lost sales

Either way, you now need to brainstorm all the relevant points you can think of under the above headings, making sure you are bringing together your knowledge from the relevant syllabus as well as your analysis of the pre-seen information.

Let's think a bit more about these requirements by breaking them down into the component parts.

It is vital that each risk has a corresponding comment on the effect i.e. to justify its inclusion in the answer as a valid point in the context of the immediate product launch.

Task 1(b)

Again you could set up headings within your answer or use a planning sheet, for example

Stage of project	*Use for Trams project*
Project ownership	– Clear ownership from the research and development team
Project responsibility	– Research and development team managing issue with prototype
Project control	– Clear testing of models throughput the development phase – Control of time, quality and cost

From your E2 knowledge, you will be aware of the way that in which projects should be managed.

Try to apply as many of your comments as possible to the fact we are talking about a mobile phone manufacturer, rather than a manufacturer of any other goods!

As a rough rule of thumb you should spend about 15–20% of the time available for reading and planning. So for this section of the exam, where you are given 45 minutes, you should be spending approximately 7–8 minutes planning your answer before you complete the exercise below. This would leave you about 35 minutes to write your answer and a few minutes spare to check through what you have written. The 35 minutes should then be allocated in line with the percentage weighting allocated to each sub-task stated within the requirement

Exercise 1
Prepare a response to the first task in the prototype exam Grainger.

4 Task 2

For task 2, the trigger and requirements are again mixed together into one screen, with the reference material shown on a separate screen:

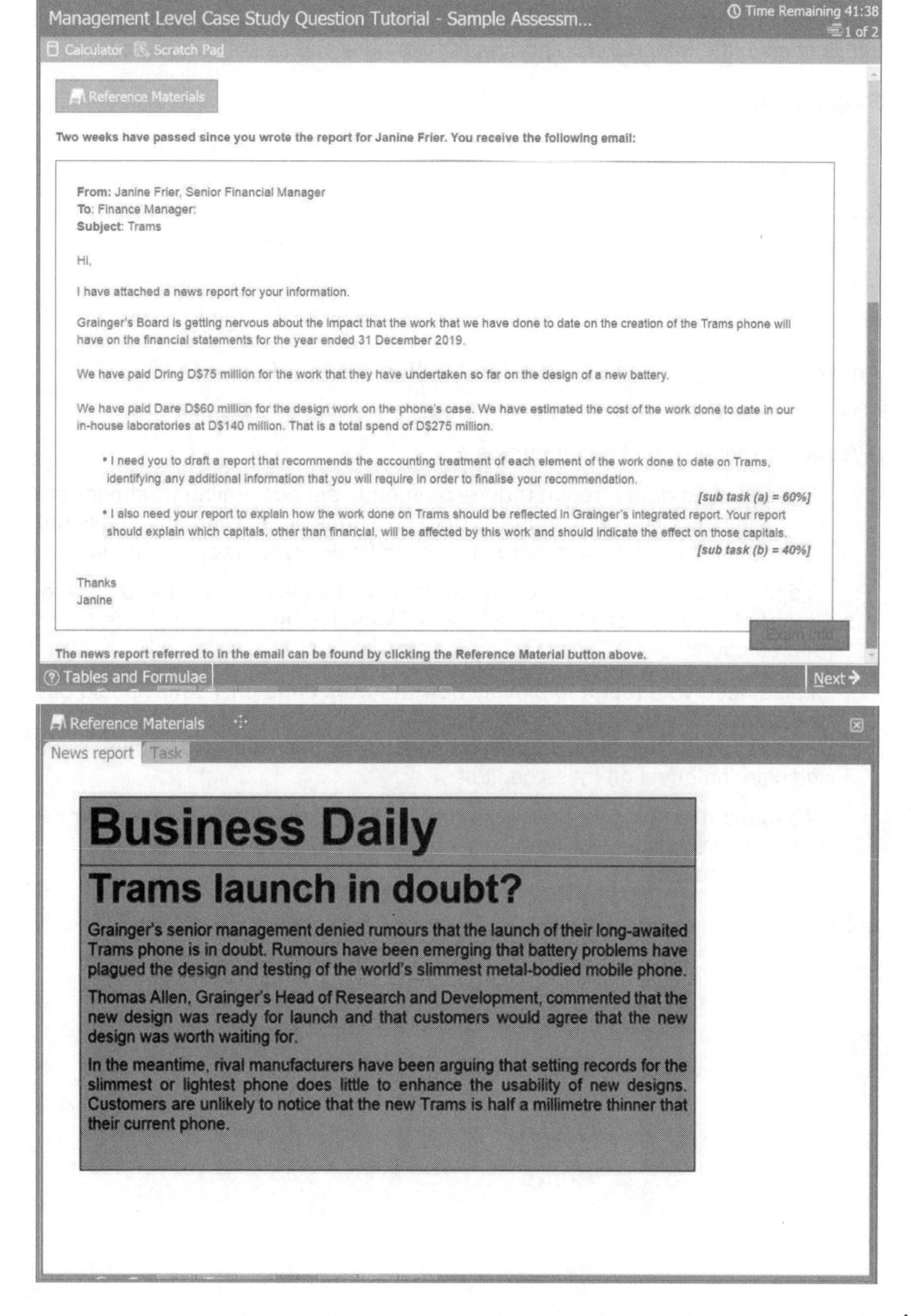

Management Level Case Study Question Tutorial - Sample Assessm...

Time Remaining 41:38

1 of 2

Calculator Scratch Pad

Reference Materials

Two weeks have passed since you wrote the report for Janine Frier. You receive the following email:

From: Janine Frier, Senior Financial Manager
To: Finance Manager:
Subject: Trams

Hi,

I have attached a news report for your information.

Grainger's Board is getting nervous about the impact that the work that we have done to date on the creation of the Trams phone will have on the financial statements for the year ended 31 December 2019.

We have paid Dring D$75 million for the work that they have undertaken so far on the design of a new battery.

We have paid Dare D$60 million for the design work on the phone's case. We have estimated the cost of the work done to date in our in-house laboratories at D$140 million. That is a total spend of D$275 million.

- I need you to draft a report that recommends the accounting treatment of each element of the work done to date on Trams, identifying any additional information that you will require in order to finalise your recommendation.

  [sub task (a) = 60%]

- I also need your report to explain how the work done on Trams should be reflected in Grainger's integrated report. Your report should explain which capitals, other than financial, will be affected by this work and should indicate the effect on those capitals.

  [sub task (b) = 40%]

Thanks
Janine

Exam Info

The news report referred to in the email can be found by clicking the Reference Material button above.

Tables and Formulae

Next

Reference Materials

News report Task

Business Daily

Trams launch in doubt?

Grainger's senior management denied rumours that the launch of their long-awaited Trams phone is in doubt. Rumours have been emerging that battery problems have plagued the design and testing of the world's slimmest metal-bodied mobile phone.

Thomas Allen, Grainger's Head of Research and Development, commented that the new design was ready for launch and that customers would agree that the new design was worth waiting for.

In the meantime, rival manufacturers have been arguing that setting records for the slimmest or lightest phone does little to enhance the usability of new designs. Customers are unlikely to notice that the new Trams is half a millimetre thinner that their current phone.

Understanding the context

With tasks like this, you still need to appreciate the bigger context before launching into the specific requirements. Within the context of the new product, we have (a) FR advice and (b) how to incorporate the work done this far into the capitals for the integrated report and any implications of the inclusion of the information in the Integrated Reporting for Grainger and its stakeholders.

Stop and think!

(1) Using your F2 knowledge, consider how should they account for the expenditure incurred thus far?

(2) You won't be expected to do complicated calculations, so what you need to answer the task should already be in the reference materials

(3) The key is to apply the syllabus knowledge to the task in hand.

(4) Can you remember the financial reporting rules for intangible assets?

Answering the question set – understanding the requirements

Given the above, the specific requirements are worded as follows:

"Produce a report ... that recommends

- "I need you to draft a report that recommends the accounting treatment of each element of the work done to date on Trams, identifying any additional information that you will require in order to finalise your recommendation.

  "To recommend is one of the highest level verbs (level 5) where you are to "propose a course of action" and "justify" why you have recommended such a course".

- "I also need your report to explain how the work done on Trams should be reflected in Grainger's integrated report. Your report should explain which capitals, other than financial, will be affected by this work and should indicate the effect on those capitals"

  "To **explain**" is a higher level verb that "to list". You need to **make clear** how this expenditure will be disclosed in the integrated report and the effect on the capitals.

Let's plan!

Task 2(a)

For F2 methodology type tasks the following approach is useful:

- **Explain** the method dictated by the relevant accounting standard – what is development, how does it apply to new products, what is an intangible asset etc.?
- **Apply** the method – walk through the steps above applying them to the specific context – what is eligible to be capitalised, how should such expenditure be amortised and so on?
- **Go beyond** the method and discuss wider issues – here you are asked for "additional information" but previous tasks have asked for limitations, other factors and so on.

Task 2(b)

For F2 integrated reporting tasks use the following steps:

- **Identify** the relevant capitals and explain how each would be affected. The requirement emphasises this so it must be addressed.
- **State** the rules – for example, outline the form that intellectual capital takes and all others affected other than financial.
- **Apply** the rules to the specific context – for example, how will any c the capitals be enhanced by the work completed on Trams and how the integrated report should explain the effect. If so, then what are the specific consequences for each capital?

Exercise 2
Prepare a response to the second task.

5 Task 3

As for task 2, the trigger and requirements for task 3 are mixed together into one screen, with the reference material presented in a separate screen:

Management Level Case Study Question Tutorial - Sample Assessm...

Time Remaining 44:22

1 of 2

Calculator Scratch Pad

Reference Materials Pre-seen

You submitted the report requested by Janine that evening. Next day, she asked you to accompany her to a meeting with Thomas Allen:

Thomas Allen, Head of Research and Development	"I am disappointed that the modifications to the design will mean that Trams will not have a true 48 hour battery life. We made that a major focal point when we were publicising our new phone. My engineers tell me that they could use a more expensive power management system that would reduce the battery drain and enable us to achieve the 48 hour battery life. I have brought along a costing based on us using the new power management system. In order to make a profit from this phone, we need to be able to make it for D$300.00 or less. I am hoping that the two of you will work with my engineers to reduce the total cost to meet that target."
Janine Frier *(turning to you)*	Please draft a paper for Thomas that sets out the challenges associated with his proposed target costing exercise and indicates how his engineers would be expected to contribute to it. ***[sub task (a) = 40%]***
Thomas Allen, Head of Research and Development	Before you both go, I should say that I am disappointed that Grainger's Board is ignoring the fact that the new battery that we are developing for Trams is a truly disruptive technology. If we succeed then Grainger will be able to develop new generations of phones that will run apps and process data constantly, without being constrained by battery life. I would appreciate your help because I am unsure how best to explain the implications of incorporating disruptive technologies into Grainger's business model to the Board.
Janine Frier *(turning to you)*	Your paper should also address Thomas' point about the need to consider disruptive technologies differently from established technologies when evaluating potential new products. ***[sub task (b) = 60%]***

Exam Inst.

The costing referred to by Thomas can be found by clicking on the Reference materials button above.

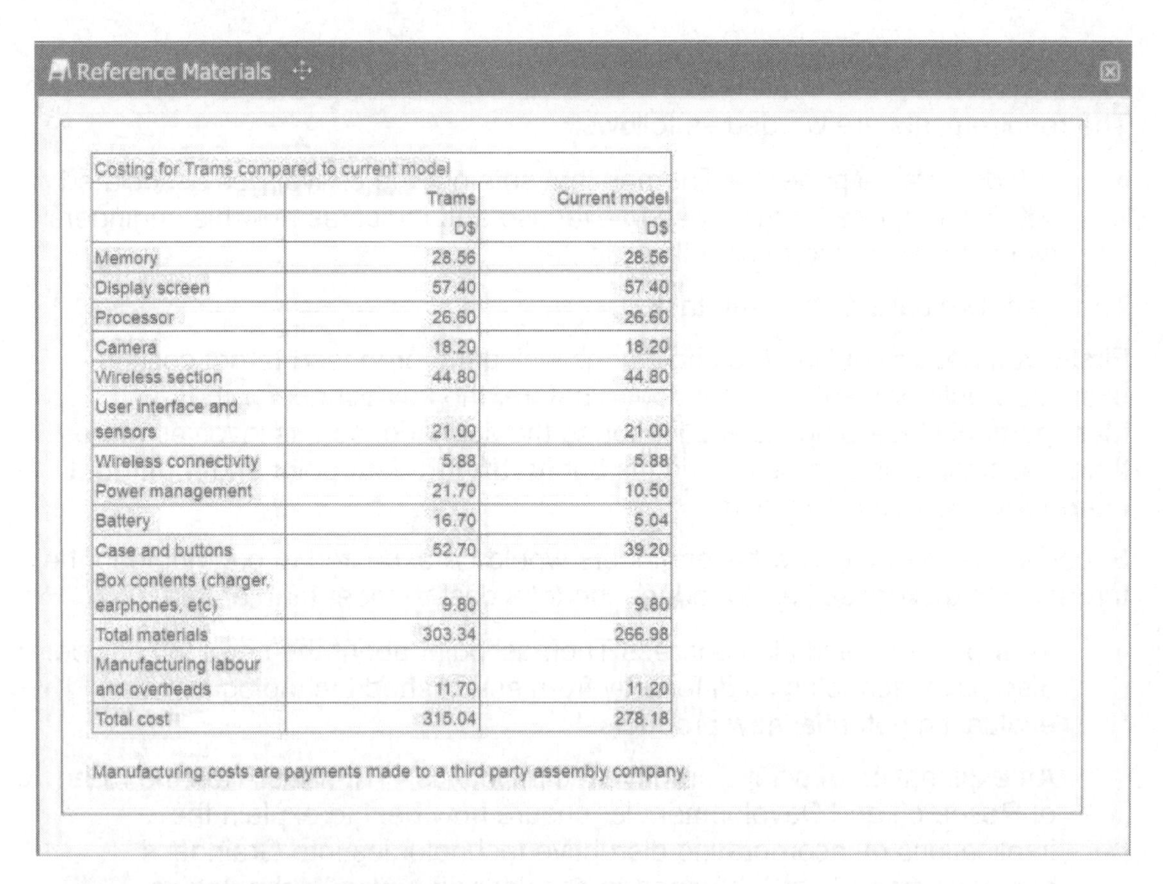

Reference Materials

Costing for Trams compared to current model		
	Trams	Current model
	D$	D$
Memory	28.56	28.56
Display screen	57.40	57.40
Processor	26.60	26.60
Camera	18.20	18.20
Wireless section	44.80	44.80
User interface and sensors	21.00	21.00
Wireless connectivity	5.88	5.88
Power management	21.70	10.50
Battery	16.70	5.04
Case and buttons	52.70	39.20
Box contents (charger, earphones, etc)	9.80	9.80
Total materials	303.34	266.98
Manufacturing labour and overheads	11.70	11.20
Total cost	315.04	278.18

Manufacturing costs are payments made to a third party assembly company.

Understanding the context

The Trams development and in particular the work on the new battery and case has highlighted the need to improve the costing methods to be sure that the new venture is profitable. Suggested improvements are to implement a target costing exercise and, for future projects, be sure that Grainger is aware and takes account of the effects of disruptive technology for new product developments. Here the context is E2 based (disruptive technology) but the specific requirements are more P2 focussed (target costing).

Also note the specific problems highlighted as you will want to ensure that you address these in your answer:

- **Additional pressure** that disruptive technology has placed on the Grainger business model.
- The **challenges** involved in the target costing exercise and how the engineers may be able to contribute.

Stop and think!

- Can you remember the principles of disruptive technology and the challenges of target costing from E2 and P2?
- Can you remember the pros and cons of target costing and disruptive technology from P2 and E2?

Answering the question set – understanding the requirements

The requirements are worded as follows:

- "Please draft a paper for Thomas that sets out the challenges associated with his proposed target costing exercise and indicates how his engineers would be expected to contribute to it.

There are two parts to this sub task:

Firstly you need to outline the challenges which the proposed target costing exercise would present. As mentioned before, the key aspect for the Management Case Study is application to the scenario, so this involves more than just stating what target costing is but **justifying** your point and **making it clear why** it will be a challenge.

Secondly you need to how his engineers would be expected to contribute to the target costing exercise i.e. "to reduce the total cost to meet that target."

- Your paper should also address Thomas' point about the need to consider disruptive technologies differently from established technologies when evaluating potential new products.

  An explanation of what disruptive technology is – Thomas Allen the Head of Research and Development is "unsure how best to explain the implications of incorporating disruptive technologies into Grainger's business model" and "the need to consider disruptive technologies differently from established technologies when evaluating potential new products"

  Although not explicitly stated, there is a clear need to **explain** (make clear) disruptive technology and its effects on the specific circumstances in Grainger.

Let's plan!

Task 3(a)

As stated in the commentary on task 2, for P2 methodology type tasks the following approach is useful:

- **Explain** the method – briefly explain what we mean by target costing and why it is relevant i.e. the need to make a saving of at least D$15.04/315.04 = 5%.
- **Apply** the method – walk through the approach and note the challenges raised and how the engineers may help.
- **Go beyond** the method and discuss wider issues – here you are asked for ideas as to how "the engineers may contribute" Your comments can be derived from a number of sources:
  - The scenario – can we secure the saving form one source or should we consider a wider range of smaller savings?

- From your P2 knowledge (e.g. target relevant costing only may be relevant to costs that have changed and many are the same between the two models – what about non-financial issues such as supplier agreements?)
- From your E2 knowledge – what are the issue with change and communication issues both with the engineers?

With all of the above try to apply your comments to Grainger as much as possible.

Task 3(b)

The same answer approach to 3(a) can be applied here:

- **Explain** the concept – briefly explain the characteristics of "disruptive technology"
- **Apply** the concept – the key aspect here is whether Grainger should switch from its current business model and incorporate disruptive technology, particularly given its effects on the mobile phone industry. Disruptive technology is relevant for some organisations but not others – how does this apply to Grainger and why?
- **Go beyond** the method and discuss wider issues – here this is incorporated into the need to consider the longer term rather focus on short term profit driven strategy.

Exercise 3
Prepare a response to the third task.

6 Task 4

As for tasks 2 and 3, the trigger and requirements for task 4 are mixed together into one screen, with the reference material presented on a separate screen:

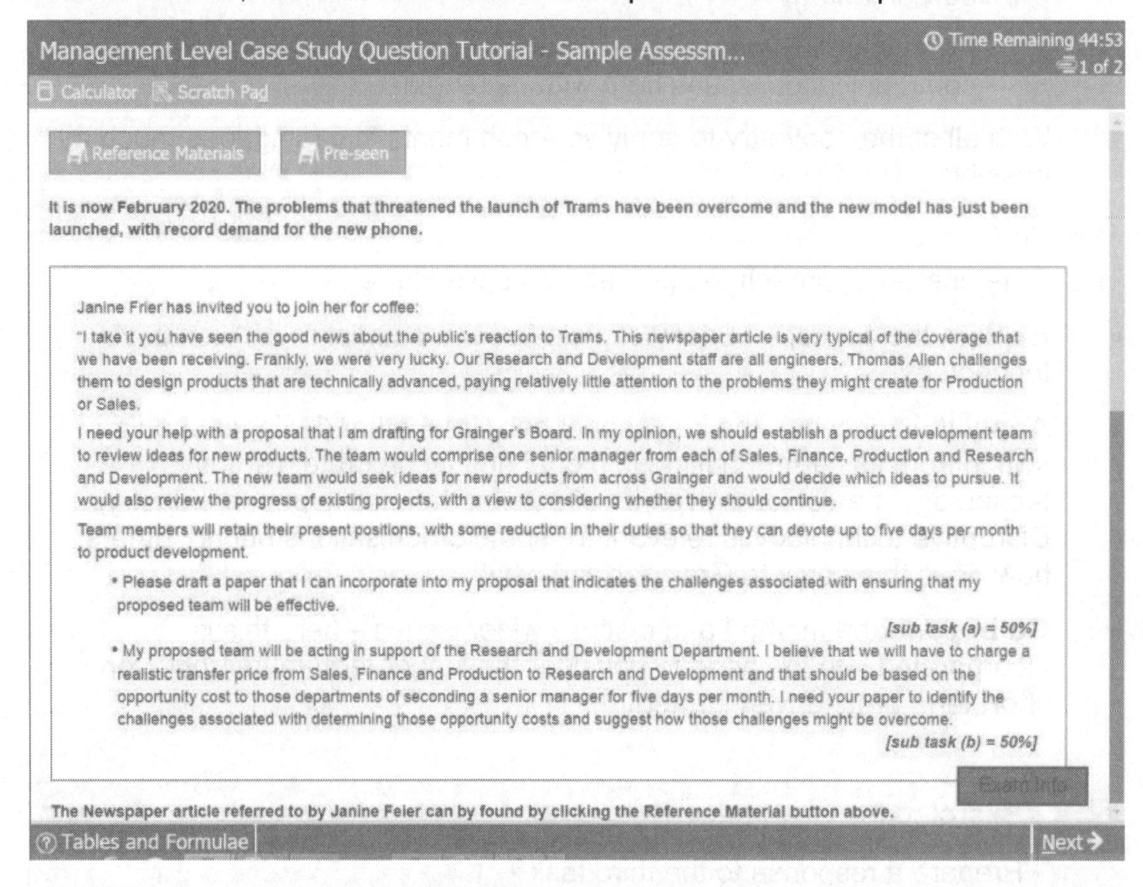

Management Level Case Study Question Tutorial - Sample Assessm...

Time Remaining 44:53

1 of 2

Calculator Scratch Pad

Reference Materials Pre-seen

It is now February 2020. The problems that threatened the launch of Trams have been overcome and the new model has just been launched, with record demand for the new phone.

Janine Frier has invited you to join her for coffee:

"I take it you have seen the good news about the public's reaction to Trams. This newspaper article is very typical of the coverage that we have been receiving. Frankly, we were very lucky. Our Research and Development staff are all engineers. Thomas Allen challenges them to design products that are technically advanced, paying relatively little attention to the problems they might create for Production or Sales.

I need your help with a proposal that I am drafting for Grainger's Board. In my opinion, we should establish a product development team to review ideas for new products. The team would comprise one senior manager from each of Sales, Finance, Production and Research and Development. The new team would seek ideas for new products from across Grainger and would decide which ideas to pursue. It would also review the progress of existing projects, with a view to considering whether they should continue.

Team members will retain their present positions, with some reduction in their duties so that they can devote up to five days per month to product development.

- Please draft a paper that I can incorporate into my proposal that indicates the challenges associated with ensuring that my proposed team will be effective.

  [sub task (a) = 50%]

- My proposed team will be acting in support of the Research and Development Department. I believe that we will have to charge a realistic transfer price from Sales, Finance and Production to Research and Development and that should be based on the opportunity cost to those departments of seconding a senior manager for five days per month. I need your paper to identify the challenges associated with determining those opportunity costs and suggest how those challenges might be overcome.

  [sub task (b) = 50%]

Exam Info

The Newspaper article referred to by Janine Feier can by found by clicking the Reference Material button above.

Tables and Formulae Next

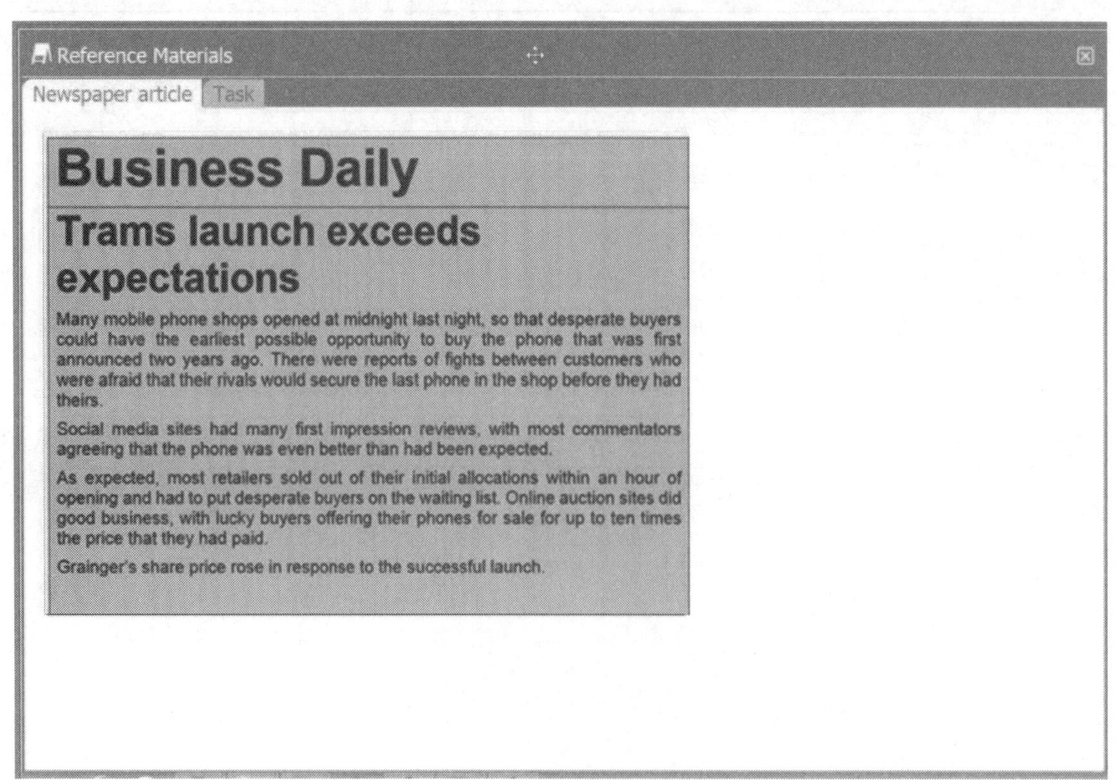

Reference Materials

Newspaper article | Task

Business Daily

Trams launch exceeds expectations

Many mobile phone shops opened at midnight last night, so that desperate buyers could have the earliest possible opportunity to buy the phone that was first announced two years ago. There were reports of fights between customers who were afraid that their rivals would secure the last phone in the shop before they had theirs.

Social media sites had many first impression reviews, with most commentators agreeing that the phone was even better than had been expected.

As expected, most retailers sold out of their initial allocations within an hour of opening and had to put desperate buyers on the waiting list. Online auction sites did good business, with lucky buyers offering their phones for sale for up to ten times the price that they had paid.

Grainger's share price rose in response to the successful launch.

Understanding the context

It is now February 2020 and the new model has been launched with great success and record sales. Based on the success of this project and associated media support, the senior financial manager is drafting a proposal for the board that they "should establish a product development team to review ideas for new products".

The new team will "seek ideas for new products from across Grainger and would decide which ideas to pursue. It would also review the progress of existing projects with a view to considering whether they should continue".

The proposed new team members "will retain their present positions, with some reduction in their duties so that they can devote up to five days per month to product development". This will inevitably lead to some internal charging between departments for services that the team carries out – i.e. transfer pricing. The proposed system will "be based on the opportunity cost to those departments of seconding a senior manager for five days per month"

Stop and think!

- Can you remember the issues with creating an effective team from E2?
- Using knowledge from P2 can you remember the issues around setting transfer prices and the challenges that this system presents?
- Can you remember what an opportunity cost is?

Answering the question set – understanding the requirements

The requirements are worded as follows:

- "Please draft a paper that I can incorporate into my proposal that indicates the challenges associated with ensuring that my proposed team will be effective".

  You have to **indicate** what the key challenges will be in forming the new team, **how** these challenges may affect the effectiveness of the team and **what** can be done to overcome these challenges to ensure that the team is effective. You must relate it to the circumstances of the case scenario, meaning that simple list of generic factors and challenges to team development is not sufficient. Your answer must make it clear the likely causes in **this** case.

- "My proposed team will be acting in support of the Research and Development Department. I believe that we will have to charge a realistic transfer price from Sales, Finance and Production to Research and Development and that should be based on the opportunity cost to those departments of seconding a senior manager for five days per month.

  I need your paper to identify the challenges associated with determining those opportunity costs and suggest how those challenges might be overcome".

You have to **identify** the challenges with determining opportunity costs and thee **suggest** how they may be overcome. It will be important therefore to note **what** the challenge is, **why** it is a challenge and then **how** you propose to resolve that challenge.

As with the previous sub task, you must relate it to the circumstances of the case scenario, meaning that simple list of challenges is not sufficient.

Let's plan!

Task 4(a)

With tasks such as this the following approach is useful:

- Briefly explain what the membership of the team will entail for each prospective member – i.e. a change to their current role and what potentially that may mean to them – for example, motivation issues, loss of promotion etc.
- For each of the challenges, how might they affect the effectiveness of the team, look for possible **causes** and what may be done to overcome these challenges

  In terms of recommendations to overcome these challenges, you can keep your answer very practical such as the importance of good communication of the purpose of the team, full support of the board etc.

Task 4(b)

To be able to overcome the challenges associated with determining opportunity costs, there is no real need to define but you could start by brainstorming as many possible issues as possible and then prioritising your list, so that you write about the 'best' ideas first. For example, suggesting that Grainger will benefit overall by the introduction of the new department so that there may be no need to instigate such a system in the first instance.

Finally try to address specific concerns over the transfer pricing system, such as to manage the resentment which the system often engenders and the effect on staff motivation etc.

Exercise 4
Prepare a response to the fourth task.

7 Summary

You should now have a better understanding of how to approach the exam requirements and plan your answer. Although this chapter uses the Question Tutorial Exam as an example, the techniques used can be applied to any set of exam tasks.

Next steps:

(1) As previously mentioned, you should attempt a written answer yourself to all of the tasks before reviewing the suggested solutions.

(2) Reviewing the solutions may highlight knowledge gaps which you may need to revisit.

(3) CIMA have produced two sample exams based on this pre-seen. You should try to attempt the second one at exam speed and using the exam software if possible.

Test your understanding answers

These answers have been provided by CIMA for information purposes only. The answers created are indicative of a response that could be given by a good candidate. They are not to be considered exhaustive, and other appropriate relevant responses would receive credit.

Answers have to be relevant and correct. Each script is marked on its merits and so a valid answer could still earn a high mark even if it takes a slightly different approach.

CIMA will not accept challenges to these answers on the basis of academic judgement.

Exercise 1

Risks associated with immediate launch

The most immediate risk is that the modifications will not work and that some of the phone will catch fire and injure customers. In everyday use, a phone catching fire could have huge consequences, such as causing a motorist to crash or threating the safety of an aircraft. Given that Grainger is aware of this risk, it will almost certainly be held liable.

Grainger's reputation will be at risk because it will be perceived as a company that puts profit before the safety of its customers. It will be very difficult to justify the decision to launch the phone without full and thorough testing. Both Dring and Dare will have incentives to make it clear that they were concerned and so the story will be very likely to become public.

There could be other problems arising from the modifications. For example, making the case out of thinner materials may make it distort and the phone may fail in the process. Releasing an unreliable product may be almost as damaging to Grainger's commercial interests as releasing a dangerous one.

There is an upside risk in that a timely launch would capitalise on market interest and consumer expectations. Any delay could lead to consumers losing interest. A delayed launch could also create the impression that there are problems with the phone's reliability.

Project management

There has been a lack of proper ownership of this project. It is unacceptable that the external design companies should be claiming to have done their individual jobs properly while the resulting parts do not fit and work together. There should have been a team within Grainger's Research and Development Department taking full responsibility for the whole project, so that the responsibility for the problems with the prototypes remained in-house.

Proper ownership would have addressed the lack of coordination between Grainger and the two outside companies. The external design companies should have been submitting samples and models to Grainger and staff there should have been checking that all dimensions were within design tolerances. Then a formal decision could have been taken as to how to rectify any compatibility issues.

The responses by the external companies imply a blame environment. Neither company could quite meet the specifications that had been imposed by the design and both attempted to deal with that by submitting a component that did not quite meet the specification.

A more constructive "no surprises" environment would have encouraged the designers to have approached the main design team at a much earlier stage to report that there were issues. Perhaps the overall design could have been modified slightly to accommodate the design problems with the battery and the case.

The short deadlines have robbed Grainger of the scope to redesign. That may have been a conscious decision because the products have a short lifecycle and there are commercial and marketing considerations, but there is little opportunity to adapt to the problems. It might have been possible to address partly by setting far stricter criteria for the designers, so that a battery that was even fractionally too large would be deemed unacceptable. That would have meant that Dare and Dring would not have tried to pass off slightly out of spec items at the last minute.

Exercise 2

Accounting treatment

The expenditure may be capitalised as development if it meets the criteria set out in IAS 38 *Intangible Assets*. The definition of development involves the application of research findings to the planning or design of new products before the start of production or use. In principle, that definition would encompass the work done on Trams because Grainger is planning to launch the new phone.

IAS 38 sets out generic criteria for the recognition of an intangible asset. Grainger will only be permitted to capitalise the costs as intangibles if it is confident that the expenditure will yield future economic benefits. It is also necessary for the cost of the asset to be determined reliably. Grainger's Board will have to consider each element of the D$275 million outlay to date separately. The IAS sets out a further set of criteria that relate specifically to development in order to apply these generic criteria. Failure of any one of those criteria would require the cost to be written off.

The D$75 million paid to Dring appears to have resulted in a viable battery design that uses new technology. If Grainger intends to proceed with the manufacture of Trams then it would be possible to capitalise the D$75 million and amortise it over the product's expected life. It may be possible to modify this treatment if the contract with Dring gives Grainger ownership of the intellectual capital in the new battery design. In that case, it may be possible to amortise it over a longer period if Grainger is confident that it will use the battery on further new products.

The D$60 million paid to Dare for the design work can only be capitalised if the Trams phone will go into production. That would require the technical problems that have affected the prototypes to be resolved and the commercial concerns voiced in the business press to be dismissed by Grainger's Board. If the phone is not expected to go into production then the design work will have little real value in itself and IAS 38 will require that it be written off.

The treatment of the D$140 million spent in-house in Grainger's laboratories will also depend on the Board's intentions to proceed with Trams. The R&D costs incurred in-house will also have to be costed accurately. It would, for example, be necessary for the design engineers to have kept records of the time spent on this particular project and for all bought-in materials and components to be traced to the development of Trams.

Integrated report

Grainger's intellectual capital will be increased by the development of this new product. The phone has design features, notably a thin case and compatible battery combination that will give the company an advantage over competitors. The report should explain the form that the intellectual capital takes, including whether it comprises contractual rights, patented products and processes and knowledge that will benefit the entity.

The creation of this new phone will also enhance Grainger's human capital by developing skills in the development of new products and in marketing the new technology. The integrated report should explain how the work done to date on Trams has helped the staff employed in the project to develop their understanding of the implementation of Grainger's strategy.

The phone has also enhanced Grainger's social and relationship capital, primarily through the work that it has undertaken with Dring and Dare, through developing the ability to work closely with those companies and through the development of an effective interface between those two key suppliers.

Grainger could also indicate the impact of this new product on natural capital. The intention behind Trams is that it will encourage customers to upgrade their mobile phones, which will lead to the unnecessary consumption of natural capital, such as scarce materials and the emissions associated with their mining and transportation. Hopefully, Grainger will be able to report some mitigation of those harmful effects.

Exercise 3

Target costing

We need to make quite a significant saving of D$15.04/315.04 = 5%. There is unlikely to be scope in saving anything on the power management component because we have just negotiated that cost. We may have to find a large number of very small savings in order to get the overall price down.

One challenge is that many of the costs appear to be the same as for our previous model. That implies that we have had these costs under review for some time and have been unable to change them. We might be able to have the engineers review those aspects that are under our direct control, such as asking whether there could be any savings in the manufacturing costs.

We should investigate the big-ticket items that have pushed the price up, such as the case. Presumably, the cases used on the old model were of an acceptable quality and so we might be able to find a way to make or buy a presentable phone case that costs a little less than D$52.70. The engineers might be asked to assist us in reengineering these parts.

Our engineers may help us to argue that the battery price is excessive because the designers at Dring did not achieve their design brief. The incremental cost of the new battery is a major part of the problem. The slim design forces us to use a bespoke battery, but we may be able to force a better price out of the supplier.

Disruptive technologies

Disruptive technologies involve the displacement of established technologies and generally brings about major change in industries. They can have the potential to create a new technology altogether. The fact that Grainger is a major manufacturer of mobile phones could mean that the company is a little too dismissive of the opportunities arising from disruptive technologies, such as the new battery.

It could be argued that the mobile phone industry is one in which the companies that take the lead in implementing and applying disruptive technologies will have an advantage over their competitors. It could be argued that most smartphones offer very similar functions and that there is very little real need for consumers to buy replacement phones. Arguably, a truly disruptive technology would have the capacity to create a desirable new product that could boost demand.

The whole point of a mobile phone is that it can operate wirelessly, powered by its internal batteries. It is well recognised that battery life is a major factor in determining how a phone can be used. If Grainger can develop expertise in a significantly improved battery technology then its mobile phones will have a massive advantage over competitors' products.

Thomas' concern appears to be that the Board is too heavily focussed on making a profit in the short term, without considering the long-term advantages that might follow on from a successful implementation of a new battery.

Thomas' basic argument appears to be that a battery with a higher capacity would do more than simply reduce the frequency with which phones had to be recharged. There would be scope for developing a new generation of apps and services that were constantly on and offering the user data and feedback. For example, the GPS tracking could be left on constantly and would measure factors such as the distance walked each day, the number of hours' sleep and so on. Thus, there would be no need to carry a fitness tracker.

Exercise 4

Effective team

Belonging to this team will involve a significant change to team members' jobs and possibly their ongoing careers. It will require them to spend roughly one day a week out of their departments, working on product development. That may lead to them being passed over for promotion because they will not be committed to their jobs.

One response to that challenge would be to seek volunteers for team membership. Ideally, team members will be motivated by their interest in product design or be looking for fresh challenges and so would be willing to accept being on a slightly different career trajectory.

There is a risk that team members will view themselves as representing their respective departments, which could create tension and lead to unhelpful discussions. This might be a particular problem for the team members from R&D, who may feel defensive about giving other departments oversight of responsibilities that were previously the responsibility of the research and development department.

The most effective response to this would be to ensure that the team is evaluated on the results that it produces, with regular reports to the Board about discussions and progress towards the development of new products. The team's convener could be the representative from R&D and he or she could be required to report directly to the Board on, say, a quarterly basis.

The nature of the team is that team members may struggle to communicate with one another, given that they will have different backgrounds and their interests in new products will be very different. The R&D representative may be the only one to understand the technical issues associated with the development of a new product and the Sales representative may be the only one who understands the marketing issues.

This challenge might be addressed by insisting that communication is informal and focusses on the commercial issues rather than the underlying technical matters. For example, if Finance produces a discounted cash flow analysis, it will be presented and explained in a manner that will be readily understood by colleagues from non-accounting backgrounds.

Opportunity cost

It could be argued that the opportunity cost of diverting senior managers will be borne by Grainger overall rather than the individual departments that they represent. If, say, the work done by Sales is less effective because a senior manager has been working on product development rather than marketing then the impact on revenue will affect the entity as a whole rather than the Sales Department.

It may be difficult to measure the opportunity cost to individual departments because that may be a simple matter of reallocating duties, with more routine work being passed down the department. For example, an assistant might be asked to take over responsibility for the preparation of a routine report and an aspect of the assistant's work passed down to an intern. The cost to the department could be minimal, especially if the team members choose to retain most of their present responsibilities and simply work harder or more efficiently to carry on as before.

Any differences between the charges made by different departments could cause resentment and friction between the team members themselves. A manager whose department negotiated a higher transfer price could regard colleagues from other departments as inferior, which could undermine the effectiveness of the team. Even charging the transfers on the basis of, say, a proportion of managers' salaries could be counter-productive because team members could infer some seniority on the basis of their respective salaries.

Finally, departments might not suffer any net opportunity cost because they will benefit from having their interests represented in the product development process. For example, Production will be able to identify difficulties in manufacturing potential products and have the designs modified, or even abandoned altogether on the grounds that they would be too difficult to make. The Departments could actually benefit from the secondment of those managers and so it may be regarded as illogical that they are being compensated by an internal charge.

Chapter

7

Feedback on the real exam and tips on answering tasks on the more technical aspects of P2 and F2

Chapter learning objectives

- To understand how to answer exam tasks that focus on the more technical areas of F2 and P2.

1 Summary of exams to date

1.1 Examiner's feedback

After each exam sitting CIMA publish the unseen examination materials, suggested answers, summary marking guides and an examiner's report that discusses all forms from that sitting.

While many students are producing high quality scripts in the time available, there are common themes that have arisen where students can improve. Here are some typical comments:

- **Time pressure is not the main problem**

  "There was little evidence that time pressure caused any problems and most candidates completed answers for all tasks, although in some of the variants answers on specific elements of tasks were superficial or too brief... Often this seemed to be due to a lack of technical knowledge..."

- **No need for lengthy introductions**

  "Some candidates are wasting time giving extraneous information. There were often lengthy introductions to issues given which then meant that there was less time to address the actual task in hand. There are no marks for introductions or setting the scene; candidates need to address the task being asked and no more."

- **Planning answers is important**

  "When sitting a Management level case study examination, it is important to take time to plan your answer so that you are able to apply your knowledge to the specifics of the case. I would suggest that for certain tasks you plan your answers in the answer screen itself.

  For example, if you are asked for the potential benefits and problems of a course of action, I would suggest that you first note down headings for benefits and problems. Then under each heading list your benefits and problems; these will become your sub-headings. Then you can write a short paragraph under each sub-heading.

  This will allow you time to think about all of the points that you want to make and will help to give your answer a clear format. Ultimately, it should save you time".

- **Apply models to the scenario**

  "There was evidence in a number of the variants of the erroneous use of learned models. In a case study the most important thing to do is to answer the task asked within the context of the business. The random inclusion of models with no application to the company, earned no marks."

- **Justify comments made**

  "Candidates also need to be conscious of unsupported assertions. Making statements such as, "this improves decision making", "this graph is essential" or "planning is enhanced" is not enough to gain any marks. Candidates must explain "how" the model or technique achieves these assertions. Wild enthusiasm is not enough without sound and reasoned explanation. Many candidate answers would have been improved if they added "because of …." at the end of a sentence to explain why something is as it is."

- **Technical marks for P2 and F2 are often the biggest discriminator**

  "As is consistent with other exam sessions, the skill which was demonstrated the best was business skills, closely followed by people skills. Candidates seemed to be most comfortable using their knowledge from E2 to demonstrate applied business and people skills. Applying knowledge from P2 and especially F2 to demonstrate technical skills appeared to be more challenging."

  "Application to the scenario was generally good for tasks that linked to the E2 and P2 syllabi but often still poor in relation to F2 and the more technical aspects of P2."

2 Answering more technical aspects of F2

2.1 Introduction

As stated above, one of the main differentiators between students who pass and students who fail is answering the more technical aspects of F2 and P2.

In the next two sections we consider some examples of such tasks from the May 2019 exam.

2.2 The May 2019 exam

The pre-seen information for the May 2019 exam concerned a company called Jord Homes, a company with a reputation for the construction of high-quality, prefabricated timber-framed houses in its home country of Corvola.

Key details were as follows:

- Formed in 1966, Jord remains privately-owned with 60% of Jord's shares owned by members of the Larsson family and the remaining 40% are owned by several Corvola based institutional shareholders. Jord still operates from one factory built in 1980, where the manufacturing facilities, showroom and head office are all still currently based.
- The business currently employs approximately 250 staff, mostly based at the factory site but due to the nature and location of the final construction work, Jord also employs teams of expert builders, tradespeople and landscapers.

- In recent years fuelled by continuous technological developments, favourable international governmental regulations in building construction, growing populations and the drive for sustainable housing the market for the prefabricated house industry has continued to grow and, as a result, the industry has seen considerable growth in the number of competitors.
- Jord's quality approach, professionalism, focus on sustainability and critically the constant and transparent liaison with the customer throughout the stages of the construction process are core to its competitive advantage and continued success.
- Based on this reputation, customers are willing to wait up to a year to own a Jord house, designed and built exclusively for them.
- With the majority of its revenue derived from Corvola is it essential that Jord has up to date and accurate information to facilitate crucial decisions surrounding its customers, range of products and services, market presence and related current capacity issues.

  Similarly, across the world there is increasing recognition of the benefit of prefabricated housing as an alternative to traditional housing and the market is, as a result, growing significantly.

  This is also likely to be applicable to other expansion opportunities either in neighbouring and/or other countries. Despite a market presence in North America and Europe, careful decisions will need to be made regarding the future direction of the business.

Taking all these factors together, it could be argued that Jord Homes was in serious need of new facilities to support the growth opportunities.

2.3 Variant 1 – section 4 – accounting for leases

Scenario

- The company decided to invest in new production premises.
- Development has commenced on "Site Two" and the Finance Director has asked for advice on how to account for the new machinery leased during the expansion.

Task

Students were asked to produce advice on the following:

(1) Via an email from the Finance Director (with a supporting email from the CEO as reference material) requesting advice on "whether it would be acceptable to account for our new machines through the statement of profit and loss only, and not capitalise them in the statement of financial position with their associated liability".

Suggested answer approach/structure

As stated in chapter 6, for F2 methodology type tasks the following approach is useful:

- **Explain** the method dictated by the relevant accounting standard
- **Apply** the method – walk through the steps above applying them to the specific context
- **Go beyond** the method and discuss wider issues

1 Explain the method

- Start with technical knowledge – **explain** what the standard states. Comments could include:

  "IFRS 16 requires that leases be accounted for on the basis of their economic substance rather than their legal form".

  "Unlike previous standards, IFRS 16 does not permit any discretion over the interpretation of the lease agreement.".

  "IFRS 16 requires that the present value of the future lease payments be calculated at the start of the lease and for the present value to be capitalised as an asset and a liability".

  "The asset will appear under PPE and the liability will be split between current and non-current liabilities, depending on whether they are due within or after 12 months".

2 Apply the method

- Then **apply** this to Jord FCB using the scenario provided.

  This is the most important aspect:

  "Jord will not own these assets in a legal sense, but it will control them for the duration of the lease".

  "The fact that a lease has been signed requires that the value of the lease should be capitalised, with the asset being depreciated over the shorter of the lease term and the asset's useful life"

3 Develop your answer

- Try to **develop points** further by considering wider issues, implications and so on.

  "The treatment of all leases in the same manner is due to the need to eliminate opportunities for the distortion of the financial statements through creative accounting"

  "If Jord could be permitted to have the lease flow through the statement of profit or loss, as Theo wishes, then the shareholders could be misled as to the company's true financial position".

Examiner's comments

Good answers outlined that an organisation cannot simply choose to account for and disclose items in a certain way in order to make things simple for the organisation and that they should use the relevant accounting standards to make such decisions. Better answers talked about the correct approach and may note the ethical implications of accounting and disclosing things incorrectly.

Students were given credit for referring to IAS17 and the distinction between operating and finance leases and were also given credit for a discussion based on IFRS16. Some credit was given if neither standard is referred to as long as the treatment of the lease is correct. This question was done quite well by most candidates.

Tutorial note:

The case was sat at a time when many candidates would have been familiar with the older accounting standard and that they were not penalised at that time.

2.4 Variant 2 – section 3 – revenue recognition on contracts

Scenario

- Jord has been asked to tender for Phase I of a proposal to build a luxury hotel on the Vorsan Golf Resort, which is located in the south European country of Marlia and later, Phase II of the proposal, should it go ahead..
- You have just received the following email from the Finance Director following a presentation she made to members of staff regarding the proposal. The Production Scheduling Manager who attended the presentation has some concerns.
- Students were given an email from the Finance Director, a supporting email from the Production Scheduling Manager to the FD.

Task

Students were then asked to explain to the Production Scheduling Manager:

(1) how and when the sales revenue from this contract would be recognised in the financial statements.

NB there was a second aspect to the task that looked at the benefit of using the time value of money in decision making but we will focus on the F2 aspects here.

Suggested answer approach/structure

As stated above for F2 methodology type tasks the following approach is useful:

- **Explain** the method dictated by the relevant accounting standard
- **Apply** the method – walk through the steps above applying them to the specific context
- Go beyond **the method and discuss wider issues**

1 Explain the method

- Start with technical knowledge – **explain** what the standard states.

  Comments could include:

  "...accounting for the delivery of the Vorsan project, we would need to consider the application of IFRS 15 – Revenues from Contracts with Customers (formerly covered by IAS 18), to determine how we account for the revenues received in the Vorsan Golf Resort project".

  "...to ensure that the financial statements reflect a position that is as close to reality as possible, leading with the matching concept".

  "...to satisfy this we must make sure that the following criteria are met: firstly, the amount of revenue can be measured reliably; secondly, it is probable that the economic benefits will flow to us; thirdly, the stage of completion at the balance sheet date can be measured reliably; and fourthly, the costs incurred, or to be incurred, in respect of the project can be measured reliably.

2 Apply the method

- Then **apply** this to Jord FCB using the scenario provided.

  This is the most important aspect:

  "The accounting issue for the Vorsan project is therefore when the revenue and costs associated with a longer-term contract should be recognised"

  "The nature of this project may be different from most of our bespoke house building projects because it will span more than one accounting period"

  "In terms of the accounting treatment of the Vorsan project, if we can estimate the outcome of the contract reliably, then the revenues and costs should be recognised in the income statement by reference to the stage of completion of the contract activity at the reporting date".

3 Develop your answer

- Try to **develop points** further by considering wider issues, implications and so on.

  "To some extent, this revenue recognition issue currently occurs with our manufacturing of homes but it is to a much lesser extent than this contract

  ..."phase I is likely to cause less difficulty for us and we should be able to simply account for Revenue as Total contract revenue × % complete', cost of sales as 'Total expected contract costs × % complete'"

  ..." phase II is contingent on factors outside of our control...prudent to not recognise this phase of the project at all until there is certainty that this will occur".

Examiner's comments

Secondly candidates were asked to explain how and when the sales revenue for the contract would be recognised in the financial statements.

This section was poorly attempted. Better candidates correctly considered the application of IFRS 15 and explained the criterion which needs to be met in order to recognise revenue. Weaker scripts showed a lack of technical knowledge, with some candidates explaining that all the revenue could be recognised as soon as the contract is signed, before any work is carried out.

3 Answering more technical aspects of P2

3.1 Introduction

As stated above, one of the main differentiators between students who pass and students who fail is answering the more technical aspects of F2 and P2.

In the last section we considered some F2 tasks from the May 2019 exam. Here we look at some P2 tasks from the same exam that caused particular difficulties for candidates.

3.2 Variant 1 – section 3 – explain the investment appraisal decision

Scenario

- Jord has selected site two for development.
- One of the institutional investors disagrees with the decision via an email to the CEO saying that they thought we should have chosen Site One because it needed less investment and that two of the three investment appraisal measures were better than for Site Two.

- Students were also provided with reference material detailing the figures that had been prepared by the Finance Director – see below

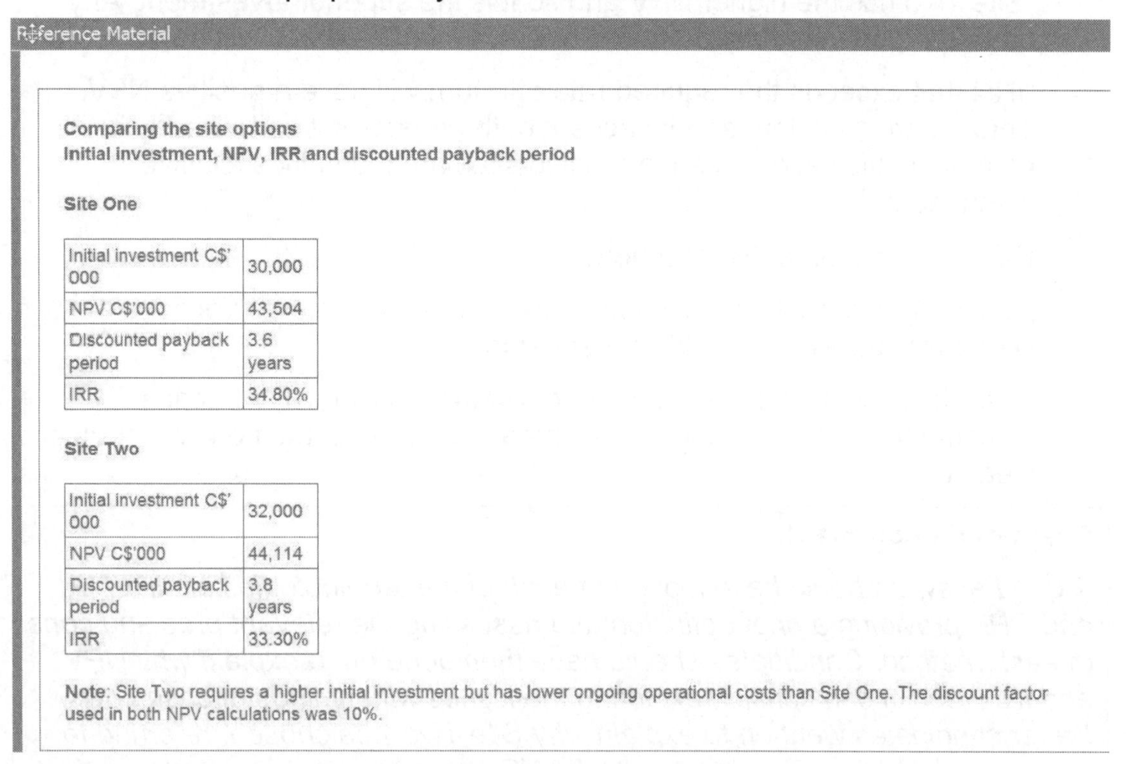
Reference Material

Comparing the site options
Initial investment, NPV, IRR and discounted payback period

Site One

Initial investment C$' 000	30,000
NPV C$'000	43,504
Discounted payback period	3.6 years
IRR	34.80%

Site Two

Initial investment C$' 000	32,000
NPV C$'000	44,114
Discounted payback period	3.8 years
IRR	33.30%

Note: Site Two requires a higher initial investment but has lower ongoing operational costs than Site One. The discount factor used in both NPV calculations was 10%.

Task

Students were asked to produce an email for the CEO on the following:

(1) can forward to the investor that explains why, from a financial perspective, Site Two is the correct choice and explains the relevance of each of the three measures Carla calculated.

Suggested answer approach/structure

Set up headings as suggested by the question requirement i.e. NPV, IRR and discounted payback period.

- Technical knowledge.

  Comments could then include:

  Provide a brief definition and assessing the relevant pros and cons of each method.

  "NPV is the only criterion that directly measures the impact of a decision on shareholder wealth"

  "IRR measures the return that is being earned on the funds invested in the project. Any project that has an IRR that exceeds the required rate of return will have a positive NPV"

  "The discounted payback of Site One is shorter, but that does not necessarily make it a better investment".

- Application.

  "Site Two has the higher NPV and so it is the superior investment. Any counterarguments based on IRR or discounted payback will be confusing".

  "IRR that exceeds the required rate of return will have a positive NPV. That means that Jord should accept both projects if it can. Clearly it cannot, in this case, because the two sites are mutually exclusive investments"

- Further development/implications

  "...Clearly it cannot, in this case, accept both investments because the two sites are mutually exclusive investments"

  "...a more rapid payback does not outweigh a larger NPV because discounted payback is not a direct measure of the impact on shareholder wealth"

Examiner's comments

A good answer should have looked at each of the terminologies of NPV, IRR and DPP providing a brief definition and assessing the relevant pros and cons of each method. Candidates should have then gone on to explain why NPV and IRR results can conflict, exploring the issues with timings of cash flows. Better candidates went on to explain why Site Two was chosen, referring to the superior NPV performance and why NPV as a measure is a better project evaluation technique.

Answers to this requirement were weak with many candidates just rambling on about NPV being superior and stating the weaknesses of other methods. This was a poor approach. Better answers expanded on this and applied the arguments to the case and clearly discussed why site two was selected. Answers to the case studies should always be applied to the case as low marks are awarded for theory.

4 Final tips

Finally, the examiner has given the following advice for candidates:

- **Application**

  Application to the scenario is key to achieving a good mark.

  Simply reproducing rote-learned answers or pure knowledge of a topic area will score very few, if any, marks.

  Similarly taking a scatter gun approach to an issue and commenting on everything that you know about it from a theoretical point of view will score few marks.

- **Planning**

  When sitting a Management level case study examination, it is important to take time to plan your answer so that you are able to apply your knowledge to the specifics of the case. I would suggest that for certain tasks you plan your answers in the answer screen itself.

  For example, if you are asked for the potential benefits and problems of outsourcing a particular function, I would suggest that you first note down headings for benefits and problems.

  Then under each heading list your benefits and problems; these will become your sub-headings.

  Then you can write a short paragraph under each sub-heading. This will allow you time to think about all of the points that you want to make and will help to give your answer a clear format.

  Ultimately, it should save you time.

- **The pre-seen material**

  Preparation on the pre-seen material is vital.

  Ensure that you are very familiar with the business; it is useful to have a good appreciation of the financial position the financial information, before the exam as this will help you with applying your knowledge and will save you time.

  Similarly, an awareness of the industry that the business is in will help you to think of the wider issues that might impact on decisions that you could be asked to comment on.

- **Know the syllabus content relating to each of the core activities within the blueprint**

  Each variant of the Management level case study examination will cover all core activities from the Management level blueprint.

  Make sure that you do not leave topic areas out of your preparation.

  Given previous comments in this report and other reports, it is evident that F2 knowledge and application of financial reporting standards is poor. You are encouraged to reflect on your knowledge of each of the three pillars, but particularly mindful of F2.

  Please pay special attention to this.

- **Justify your comments**

  Be prepared to give balanced arguments or appraisals.

  Quite often you will be asked whether a tool or technique is appropriate to the business – it is just as likely to be suitable as not suitable.